# K E N T

# KENT

## NIGEL NICOLSON

### PHOTOGRAPHS BY

## PATRICK SUTHERLAND

HARMONY BOOKS
NEW YORK

# Acknowledgements

In preparing this book I have visited every place described, and flown over a large part of east Kent by light plane. I have drawn upon a great number of earlier accounts by travellers and specialists, from William Lambarde in the sixteenth century to modern guidebooks. Particularly should I mention John Newman's two volumes on the buildings of Kent in the Pevsner series, Frank W. Jessup's *A History of Kent*, Marcus Crouch's *Kent*, K.P. Witney's *The Jutish Forest*, Walter J.C. Murray's *Romney Marsh*, Richard Church's *Portrait of Canterbury*, Caroline Hillier's *The Bulwark Shore*, Alan Bignell's *Kent Villages* and the annual volumes of *Archaeologia Cantiana*. My collaboration with Patrick Sutherland, who took the photographs, has been unfailingly pleasant and productive.

Copyright © 1988 by Nigel Nicolson

Published by Harmony Books, a division of Crown Publishers, Inc.

225 Park Avenue South, New York, New York 10003
Published in Great Britain by George Weidenfeld & Nicolson Limited

HARMONY and colophon are trademarks of Crown Publishers, Inc.

Manufactured in Italy

Library of Congress Cataloging-in-Publication Data
Nicolson, Nigel.
 Nigel Nicolson's Kent.
 1. Kent—Description and travel.   I. Title.
DA670.K3N53  1988   914.22′304858   87–18143
ISBN 0-517-56858-6
10 9 8 7 6 5 4 3 2 1
First Edition

# Contents

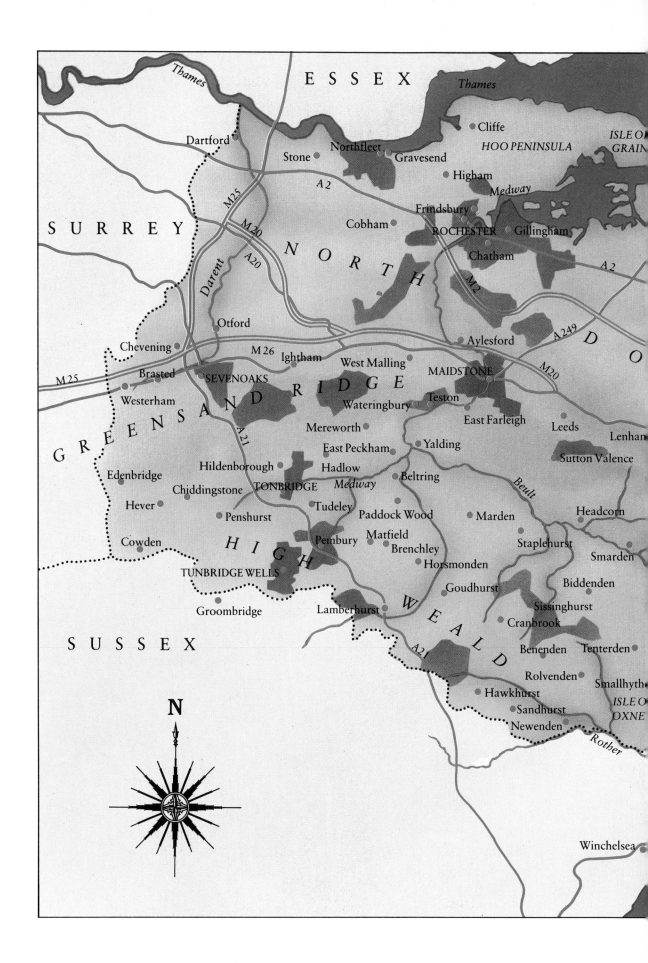

NORTH SEA

Sheerness
Minster
Queenborough
ISLE OF SHEPPEY
SITTINGBOURNE
Swale
Faversham
M2
A299

HERNE BAY
Reculver
St Nicholas at Wade
Sarre
A28

MARGATE
NORTH FORELAND
Broadstairs
ISLE OF THANET
RAMSGATE
Minster
PEGWELL BAY
Richborough

Stour

Fordwich
Ickham
CANTERBURY
Wingham
Sandwich

W
N
S
Chilham
Great Stour
Kingston
Goodnestone

Charing
A28
Godmersham
Barfreston
Deal
Walmer

A20
Wye
Little Stour
A2
St Margaret's at Cliffe

ASHFORD
Hinxhill
Elham
SOUTH FORELAND
DOVER

Lympne
A259
FOLKESTONE

Royal Military Canal
Hythe

Appledore
ROMNEY MARSH
Dymchurch

Fairfield
A259
St Mary's Bay

Old Romney
New Romney
Littlestone

WALLAND MARSH
Rye
Lydd

STRAIT OF DOVER

Dungeness

# Foreword

THIS IS NOT A GUIDEBOOK, nor is it a history. It is a combination of the two, and aims to describe how Kent came to look the way it does. It explains what the county has endured and achieved by invasion and counter-attack; how chance, invention, art, fortitude and much labour have fashioned its countryside, buildings, defences, industries and communications; how the happy division between its urban and rural parts has been retained, the relationship between the ports and inland towns, and the influence of the metropolis and Kent's contribution to it. It is in short a study, by someone who has lived in Kent for much of his life, of how a very specially endowed and located part of England has survived threats, internal and external, which might have rendered it a suburb, an armed camp, a corridor or a vast industrial estate, but haven't.

Agriculture and de-afforestation played an obvious part in transforming a naturally rich soil into the Garden of England, but there are other parts of the country equally favoured which never became so fecund or wealthy as Kent. There are several reasons for this. The county is bordered to the north by the Thames, which leads in one direction to the capital and in the other opens conveniently opposite the main river mouths of northern Europe. It is split down the middle by another river, the Medway, which from its earliest history made the hinterland accessible. The North Downs provided from prehistoric times an all-weather trackway from east to west. Thus Kent already possessed natural communications for its travellers and products long before the full development of its roads, and the biggest market in the country lay within easy reach. Kent became London's larder. It benefited, further, from the wealth of Canterbury, where the religious capital of England was established for the sole reason that St Augustine found there a sympathetic king. Because of Canterbury, the proximity of both London and the ports, and the growing beauty of the county, rich merchants and clerics, and even the Court itself, chose to develop estates here and to build the great houses and churches which still adorn the land.

*The South Foreland and
St Margaret's Bay, where there
is a break in the cliffs and a steep
road leads down to the beach.
Withdrawn from the cliff top is
the village of St Margaret's at
Cliffe, with one of the finest
Norman churches in the county.*

From the sixteenth century onwards another benefit accrued to Kent. The lower reaches of the Medway and its estuary were favourable sites for building, repairing and berthing the Fleet, and round Chatham and Sheerness rose the great dockyards, and with them the fortifications necessary for their defence. It was not until the nineteenth century that industry began to extend along the Thames, and then it spread very rapidly, giving Kent a wholly new source of employment and creating out of riverside villages a chain of towns from Sittingbourne to Dartford that increased and concentrated the population amazingly. At the same time the rim of Thanet became the most popular holiday resort for Londoners and led to a coagulation of seaside towns almost unbroken from Whitstable to Ramsgate.

Thus a purely agricultural county became in response to new opportunities and demands a thriving maritime, industrial and recreational base. But the wonder of Kent is that it has preserved unmarked by industry or tourism its ancient heartland south of the Downs. The Weald, which occupies with Romney Marsh a third of the county, is to this day a region of small towns, scattered villages and farms. This fortunate accident had nothing to do with its remoteness for, since the felling of the Wealden forest in the early Middle Ages, it has been reasonably accessible, and later the railways spread to every part of it. It is due to a deep agricultural tradition and to planning legislation which came just in time. Other parts of Kent, like that enclosed by the triangle formed by Dover, Canterbury and Ashford, have remained remarkably empty, unspoiled and unknown, in spite of the discovery of coal there in 1891.

Kent has the good fortune to be separated into mutually independent parts. The old division between Kentish Men and Men of Kent (the dividing line was the Medway, with Kentish Men to the west) was never anything more than a legend, and certainly never implied any animosity between the two. The county's geography is in part responsible for its diversity. It forms a jigsaw made of a few large pieces. The rivers are not the boundaries between them: three of them, the Medway, the Stour and the Darent, flow paradoxically, breaking northwards through the Downs against the grain of the country because they existed long before the dome of chalk subsided to form the transverse valley, and the Rother slips separately into the Channel at Rye. The divisions are shaped by the North Downs and the parallel ridge of greensand (which surprisingly, considering it is so prominent a feature of central Kent, has never been given a local name), by the low-lying coastal lands, much reclaimed from the sea, by the broad shelf along the southern bank of the Thames, and by the former great forest of the Weald.

Each of these districts has developed its special character. Familiar though one may be with Kent, it rewards the traveller with constant surprises. It was by accident that I found a delectable valley unknown to me, running east from Hollingbourne to Doddington and Newnham north of the Downs, hidden villages like Wickhambreaux near Canterbury, and Harty church in remotest Sheppey. Such places are visual evidence that the land has been treated with much affection. The character of the countryside has been shaped by farms averaging a hundred and fifty acres, sometimes sixty to a parish. Every open space has been cultivated. There is no wasteland in Kent and scarcely a swamp; there are no moors, no unmanageable hills, no impenetrable woods though one-eighth of the county is still woodland. The Downs do not roll bare and majestically like the Sussex Downs to Beachy Head for, except near Wye and above Folkestone, they shelve northwards into huge fields of corn. Away from the estuaries and larger towns the landscape is still basically medieval, and has changed far less than most Midland counties, where a majority of farm sites are no older than the eighteenth or nineteenth centuries. In Kent, writes Professor A.M.Everitt in a recent study of its agrarian history, 'there are probably about ten thousand farms and hamlets whose sites have been continuously occupied for the best part of eight hundred years, and in many cases for a very much longer period', and he estimates that some eight thousand medieval buildings survive. Almost every village existed embryonically before the Norman Conquest, and only one inland town, Tunbridge Wells, is the creation of the last three centuries.

The marshes, which are no longer marshes, have been described in this account as a group because their reclamation is quite a separate story, though Romney Marsh and the low-lying parts of Thanet, Sheppey and the Hoo peninsula have many distinguishing characteristics. The northern industrial zone is given its own chapter, and so is the Weald, to complete the jigsaw. This leaves the two cities, Canterbury and Rochester, the towns and the major country houses. I have not hesitated to be selective, to praise and sometimes abuse, for Kent has undoubted eyesores especially along the coasts, nor to nominate my favourites: among towns, Sandwich, Rochester and Lydd; among villages, Lenham and Matfield; among the larger houses, Penshurst and Broome Park; among churches, Goudhurst, Cobham and St Margaret's at Cliffe; and among modern buildings the power station on the Isle of Grain. If the industrial towns are treated scantily, it is because they are loved more by their inhabitants than by visitors.

Kent has made a major contribution to the country's defences. Inevitably so, because it is

> A soil that doth advance
> Her haughty brow against the coast of France,

and its shores are festooned with castles and other barricades. Conversely, it has always been Britain's peaceful route to the Continent. Its major ports, Dover, Folkestone and now Ramsgate, are artificial, since no estuary faces the nearest shore of France. The Channel Tunnel, to which I have devoted several pages in anticipation, will make an impact on the county even greater than the industrialization of its northern shore, or the completion of the M25 round London and the two other motorways which link it to the ports. But Kent is as carefully guarded against contamination as it was immemorially against invasion, and I take the side of the optimists.

# I

# The Coast and its Defences

THE POINT WHERE Julius Caesar landed in August 55 BC cannot be exactly determined because his *Commentaries* name no place names except that of Kent itself, *Cantium*, and *Tamesis*, the Thames, but it was probably the beach between Deal and Walmer. Not the beach we see today, for the shoreline has shifted in these two thousand years, but similar to it, pebbly and quite steeply sloping. Caesar describes how his fleet manoeuvred off Dover, and finding the cliffs too formidable a bulwark and lined by a yelling crowd of Britons, he turned north for seven miles and selected almost the first open beach he came to. Had he gone another mile or two he would have discovered the natural harbour of Richborough at the mouth of the Wantsum, the channel which then separated Thanet from the mainland. His ignorance of its existence reveals the Romans' surprising unfamiliarity with a coastline visible from Gaul, with which the natives had been trading for centuries.

The Britons had followed the invading fleet along the cliff top and were already in position with cavalry and war chariots to oppose the landing. Caesar describes the scene:

> The troops were loaded with the great weight of their arms, and had to leap down from their vessels, stand firm in the waves, and fight the enemy who advanced a little way into the water and boldly hurled their missiles or spurred on their horses ... Then, as our troops still hung back, chiefly on account of the depth of the sea, the eagle-bearer of the Tenth Legion cried, 'Leap down, soldiers, unless you wish to betray your eagle to the enemy. It shall be told that I at any rate did my duty to my country and my general.' With that, he cast himself forth from the ship and began to bear the eagle against the enemy. Then our troops exhorted one another not to allow so dire a disgrace, and leapt down from the ships with one accord.

There was fierce fighting in the surf, but as soon as the first legionaries gained firm ground they charged in a body and occupied a small eminence, perhaps the hump on which Walmer Castle now stands. The pursuit was inconclusive because Caesar's cavalry had

*Previous page: A placid scene in Dover harbour, a port since Roman times, when it lay at the mouth of the Dour, a small river. As the closest port to France, Dover grew in importance and, when the estuary silted up, the artificial harbour increased in size. In 1909 the breakwaters could contain the entire British Fleet. The first car-ferries were introduced in the 1950s, and for freight and passengers it is still by far the busiest of Kent's ports.*

*The famous chalk cliffs have become a symbol – in history, literature and song – not only of England's welcome to the traveller, but often also of her defiance. The cliffs run for no more than thirteen miles, from Folkestone through Dover to Deal, and it was from the rolling Downs above them that the Britons first sighted Caesar's approaching fleet.*

not managed to cross from Boulogne, but the Britons supinely sent emissaries to sue for peace.

The Romans hurriedly threw up a fortified camp, of which no trace has been discovered, perhaps because it lay beyond the present low-water mark. Then they suffered a setback which almost ended the expedition before they had moved a mile inland. A storm which had scattered the cavalry transports smashed Caesar's ships to pieces, some as they lay drawn up on the beach like today's fishing boats at Deal, others riding at anchor a little way offshore. The army, two legions and some auxiliaries, about twelve thousand men in all, were cut off from their base in France, and they had brought with them no provisions, as nothing but a reconnaissance in force had been intended. As Caesar continues,

> When they became aware of this the British chiefs who had assembled at our headquarters after the fight took counsel together. As they knew that the Romans lacked cavalry, ships and corn, and perceived the scantiness of the army from the smallness of the camp . . . they decided to renew the war and prolong it into the winter . . . . Departing a few at a time from the camp, they began secretly to draw in their followers from the fields.

In this desperate situation Caesar ordered some of his men to forage, others to make the less damaged ships tolerably seaworthy. A large party of foragers was cut off by the British cavalry and infantrymen who had dismounted from the chariots, and their plight was grave enough for Caesar to intervene in person with a relieving force that drove the enemy a few miles off. That was the end of the 'invasion'. Taking hostages, the Roman army limped back to Boulogne. It had been a fiasco, redeemed only by Caesar's quick reactions and the honesty with which he recorded it. He had a reputation for getting his men out of the messes he got them into.

When he returned to Britain the following year, this time with five legions and two thousand horse, he chose paradoxically the same beach, and though his eight hundred transports were now made shallow draft to run more easily ashore, he suffered the same penalty. All his ships were again badly damaged by a storm, forty of them irreparably. His landing had been unopposed. The Britons, terrified by the sight of so huge a fleet, withdrew to a hill-fort, now confidently identified with Bigbury, two miles west of Canterbury, where to this day you can trace, when the wood is coppiced, the low

*Kingston emerges from the mist which fills the folds of the rolling country between the coast and Canterbury. The village lies on the route taken by Caesar in 54 BC, on his famous night march to attack the British levies at Bigbury.*

*Aylesford, situated on the lowest ford of the Medway, is perhaps the longest inhabited settlement in Kent, and it is also the place where Hengist and Horsa defeated Vortigern in AD 455. In its parish are Neolithic, Bronze-Age and Iron-Age burial grounds. The church tower is Norman, except for its upper stage, and the bridge is medieval.*

outlines of steep earthen banks. Caesar immediately, and by night, led the major part of his army twelve miles cross-country to attack it. There is nothing in his account to tell us how he discovered the direction or the way. He records only that his advance was opposed at the crossing of the Stour below the camp, and having forced it, stormed the single rampart and captured it with few casualties. It was then that he received news of the damage to his ships. He hurried back to Deal and set his men to repair those that could be salvaged. He then returned to Bigbury, where there was further fighting, part pitched, part guerilla, in which the legions soon won the upper hand. Caesar advanced to the Thames, crossed it under fire, possibly at Brentford, and continued as far as the neighbourhood of St Albans, where he destroyed the capital town, governed by Cassivelaunus, the first named Briton in our history, under whom all the south-eastern levies had agreed to serve in the emergency. Having won all his battles but accomplished nothing permanently, Caesar withdrew to the Continent. Britain was left in peace for the next hundred years.

What was the condition of Kent and Kentishmen during the

period of these futile probes? The part of the county which Caesar traversed during that famous night march and subsequent advance differed greatly in detail from what we see today, but its structure was the same – the cliffs and beaches, the upper Stour valley, the North Downs, the scattered woods and cultivated fields. He skirted the great Wealden forest and found the land east and north of it open enough to enable a huge army to cross it by night and the British war-chariots to wheel and manoeuvre, 'galloping their teams down the steepest slopes without loss of control', he wrote. There were of course no made roads, but prehistoric trackways, including that which came to be known as the Pilgrims' Way, linked every part of the country, and there were farmsteads in abundance, the simple buildings probably circular and thatched. 'Of all the Britons,' Caesar wrote, with odd confidence, because he had only met a handful of them, 'the inhabitants of Kent are by far the most civilized', and then contradicts himself: 'They clothe themselves in skins and dye their bodies with woad, which produces a blue colour and makes their appearance in battle more terrible.' Previous migrants from the upper Rhine and northern Gaul had brought with them the heavy plough, and they kept great herds of cattle. They mined the iron of the Weald. They knew the art of turning pottery on the wheel. They used coinage. They populated the open part of Kent thickly, for it had been colonized since the fourth century BC, chiefly along the line of the later Watling Street and in the Medway valley. By the time of Caesar's invasions the tribal areas were organized under four separate kings. They built a few primitive forts for protection against each other, like Bigbury, Oldbury (the largest) and High Rocks at Tunbridge Wells, but none so massive as the forts of the West Country, and they had no navy to harass Caesar's arrival and departure. Little survives to mark their culture. The cemeteries at Aylesford and Deal are the most productive of artefacts, and the excavation of Bigbury has disclosed the metal parts of a chariot, some household goods and iron tools, and, significantly, a slave chain. The Downs still bear traces of ancient cultivation, on steep slopes which no modern farmer would dream of ploughing.

When the Romans next set foot in Britain, in AD 43, they discovered the mouth of the Wantsum, just north of Sandwich, and constructed a temporary camp at Richborough on an island or peninsula jutting into the channel. What we see there now are the walls of a third-century fort, one corner chewed away by the Stour, but the long line of the original rampart has been excavated and part of it left exposed. From this base Aulus Plautius began his march along the North Downs and met little opposition until he reached the

*Richborough Castle* (Rutupiae), *a mile north of Sandwich, was the landing-place of the Romans in* AD 43 *and, for a time, their supply base for the conquest of Britain. The flint and concrete walls in the background, eleven feet thick, date from the late third century, when the camp was greatly enlarged by the Romans to become one of their eleven Saxon Shore Forts.*

*The oyster farm at Whitstable, where oysters have been cultivated for two thousand years.*

Medway four miles south of Rochester. On the far bank the Britons were assembled in great strength, but confidently bivouacked, says the Roman historian Dio, as they thought it impossible for the enemy to cross without a bridge. One can visualize the scene as one drives over the river on the M2, for the contours are quite unchanged. The Roman general sent two legions under the youthful Vespasian, the future Emperor, to cross the Medway two miles upstream, near Wouldham. There the mud flats offer some patches of stony ground, sufficient purchase for the cavalry, which swam across almost unnoticed to take the enemy in the flank, preceded by cohorts of Batavians swimming in full armour, while the main army demonstrated on the near bank. It was growing dark, and the battle was resumed next day, one of the fiercest and most significant fought on British soil, but there is no memorial to mark it. The Britons still had their chariots and cavalry, but their troops were untrained and ill-organized, no match for the disciplined legions, and they retreated, taking refuge in the swamps and forests in the hope that they would exhaust the invaders in fruitless pursuit. Aulus Plautius ignored them, pressed on to the Thames which he crossed perhaps at the site of London Bridge or by a ford at its estuary, and having awaited the arrival of the Emperor Claudius, he captured the British provincial capital of Colchester. The conquest of the whole of Britain followed during the next few decades.

Kent had not played a glorious part in the second Roman war. There were few local men on the Medway, which was guarded by levies from Essex and Hertfordshire. There could have been many Kentish men who actually welcomed the Roman occupation for the security it gave them, and for the rapid ramification of trade which brought unprecedented luxuries to Britain. The county was soon pacified. Alongside the native farms, which continued for centuries to be cultivated in the traditional way, there sprung up, here and there, Romanized villas. Sixty of them have been recorded in Kent, mainly in the valleys and along the lower slopes of the Downs, and the finest, at Lullingstone, is still open to view. There were only two Roman towns, Canterbury (much the larger) and Rochester, where Watling Street crossed the Stour and Medway, and it is now widely accepted by archaeologists that rural life was based on villages, much as today. Corn was the main crop, and sheep and cattle varied the scene and diet. The Channel ports were Richborough, Lympne, Dover and Reculver, and from them the Romans constructed roads to Canterbury, where Watling Street took over as the only route to London and the north-west. All of them except the Reculver road can be identified by their straightness on the map. The most remarkable on the ground is the road due north from Lympne, wonderfully rising and falling with scarcely a deviation till just

*The twelfth-century twin towers of Reculver, which balance precariously on the sea-eroded cliff-edge, are still a landmark for mariners, although they are almost all that remains of a church founded in about 670. Excavation has revealed part of the Roman fort sited here to guard the northern mouth of the Wantsum – the tidal channel separating the Isle of Thanet from the mainland.*

short of Canterbury. Other roads ran south from Rochester through Maidstone and Staplehurst to the iron mines of the Weald, with branch roads through Sutton Valence and Tenterden.

But of the Roman occupation of three and a half centuries curiously little evidence is visible. In the grounds of Dover Castle there is the stump of the lighthouse which answered to another at Boulogne, and in the town's centre the so-called Painted House has recently been excavated, a dismal group of shattered rooms dignified by the modern structure that roofs it and by the exhibition that explains it. The most dramatic Roman relics date from the final phase of the occupation, the forts of the Saxon Shore. There were eleven of them, from Brancaster in Norfolk to Porchester in Hampshire, and four, more closely grouped than elsewhere, lie on the Kentish coast – Reculver, Richborough, Dover and Lympne. They were built towards the end of the third century to defend the province against Saxon raids. All were sited on river mouths, where the garrisons could be supported by the fleet. The Dover fort has been obliterated by the modern town, and Lympne (Stutfall Castle) is marked by nothing more than a chute of Roman masonry

collapsed down the steep bank that formed the sea cliff before
Romney Marsh was drained. At Reculver one can trace half the
embankment of the camp overlooking the old channel of the
Wantsum, but the remainder was torn away by the erosion of the
cliff, leaving perilously perched above it the twin towers of the
ruined Norman church, built within the camp and preserved by
Trinity House as a guide to mariners. The finest is Richborough.
Here the Roman supply depot was greatly enlarged in about AD 280
to cover an area of ten acres. The flint and masonry walls of the
Saxon Shore fort, protected by triple ditches, stand in places to a
height of twenty-five feet, and ten to twelve feet thick. Within them,
on neatly tonsured English Heritage lawns, are the foundations of a
few buildings of different periods, including the cruciform base of a
huge monument erected in the first century to celebrate the
subjugation of Britain. It was through the western gateway, which
sturdily survives, that the legions began their long marches to
Hadrian's Wall, and through the eastern that the last of them
embarked early in the fifth century, leaving Britain to its fate.

Just north of Richborough the farm of Ebbsfleet is the site of two
of the greatest events in Kent's history. Hengist and Horsa landed

*The salt marshes on the verge of Pegwell Bay, south of Ramsgate, lie close to the place where the Saxons landed in 449, and where St Augustine came ashore in 597. After the Second World War it was one of the first areas to be designated as a Site of Special Scientific Interest (SSSI) for the preservation of its birds, flowers and insects.*

there in AD 449, and St Augustine in 597. The monument to the two Jutish kings is a beautiful reconstruction of a Viking ship, the *Hugin*, which in 1949 a crew of enterprising Danes sailed and rowed across the Channel. The monument to the saint is a simple stone cross. The shoreline here, though beneficial to marine plants and birds, is not beautiful. The flat land is dominated by the cooling towers of a vast power station, is sliced by road and railway, and straggles indecorously into Pegwell Bay. It takes much imagination to reconstruct the scene.

Hengist and Horsa were rashly invited by the Kentish king Vortigern to defend his kingdom from marauding Picts, promising them no more than Thanet as a reward. Instead, they turned on their host, fought several battles against him, in one of which Horsa was killed, and occupied southern Britain as far west as the Isle of Wight. The Romano-British population either fled or submitted to a status little superior to serfdom. This disaster left a permanent mark on Kent, to its eventual benefit. The Jutes, who came not from Jutland but more likely from the middle Rhine, were highly organized and enterprising. Their culture, of which evidence exists in the gold, silver, glass and jewellery found in cemeteries at Faversham and on Kingston Down, was uniquely splendid. Because they left no written records behind, we tend to think of them as barbarians, as hired mercenaries who ravaged a peaceful land. In fact they imposed order on the kingdom and re-established trading links between Kent and every part of the Continent as far as the Middle East. They settled the river valleys – the frequent termination '-ing' to place names, like Barming, West Malling, Yalding, marks their presence – and one should picture Kent under Jutish rule as a refinement of the countryside which the Romans had abandoned. Their laws were not harsh. The native farmers, and the Jutish veterans who settled on the land beside them, enjoyed a freedom and prosperity unequalled in any other part of Anglo-Saxon Britain. To a large extent they created the pattern of settlements which the Domesday Book describes.

So it was a Jutish king, Ethelbert, whom St Augustine found in Canterbury when he landed at Eastertime 597, sent by Pope Gregory to reclaim for Christianity 'a barbarous, fierce and unbelieving nation' who worshipped Thor and Woden. Such was Kent's reputation, undeserved, in Rome. The king welcomed the mission. His wife Bertha was the daughter of a Christian king reigning in Paris, and the old Roman chapel, St Martin's, just outside Canterbury's walls became her place of Christian worship. It was there that St Augustine held his first services, preaching through an interpreter, and today one can enter its narrow chancel, built of Roman brick, with certainty that it was on this very spot that English Christianity became firmly rooted. Ethelbert accepted baptism himself, and ten thousand Kentish people followed his example. St Augustine was consecrated 'Archbishop of the English', built Canterbury's first cathedral and the Monastery of St Peter and St Paul, and in 604, the year of his death, established a second see at Rochester. The faith spread slowly through the country. Sussex remained heathen till 680. So in this gentle way, Kent was the first of the English counties to be converted, and Canterbury gained a pre-eminence over York which it has held ever since.

In the ninth century Kent was again invaded, by the Vikings. In 839 there was great slaughter in Canterbury and Rochester, and thirteen years later a large Viking army wintered in Thanet after a big battle at Sandwich. In 865 they came again, and pressed up the coast to savage London. But the most ambitious raid was in 892, when two hundred and fifty ships set out from Boulogne and landed at New Romney, followed by eighty more which invaded Kent's northern shore. The two pincers converged, one from Appledore, the other from Milton Regis near Sittingbourne, but Alfred interposed his own army between them, at Charing, and twice defeated the Danes, whose survivors fled to Essex and Surrey. It was a considerable achievement. The English had no fleet, and scarcely any prepared defences. At Appledore, for example, there was a half-completed fortlet (of which no trace remains) manned by a handful of peasants. Alfred succeeded in preventing any permanent settlement in Kent, where there are no Viking relics and no place names to commemorate their violent passage through it, and although several towns were sacked and battered, the raids had little lasting effect upon the life of the country people.

It was with the same placid resignation that the county accepted the Norman Conquest. William landed at Pevensey in Sussex, a detachment having been repelled at Romney, and after Senlac made his way to Dover, which surrendered without a fight. He allowed Kent to retain its traditional liberties under its new feudal masters, confirming Saxon rights in their antique language, granting the manor of Wye, for instance, 'freedom from Geld and Scot and Hidage and Danegeld, Sac and Soc and Thol and Theam and Infangenthef, and War and Wardpenny and Lastages and Hamsoken and Forstal and Bloodwite and Childwite', a wide-sweeping enumeration of ancient dues which so puzzled the Norman lawyers that they cancelled the lot.

The most important of the customs which were preserved, peculiar to Kent, was Gavelkind, a legal obligation to divide among all his sons equally the holdings of a landlord who died intestate. It was not finally abolished till 1925. It resulted in constant subdivision of the land, each part freehold, of which the present evidence is

*Barfreston, a tiny village in the hidden country north-west of Dover, has one of the best-known Norman churches in the county. The south door is richly carved: fighting animals and signs of the zodiac surround a seated Christ in the centre.*

that there is scarcely a place from which two or more farms cannot be seen, although by purchase and amalgamation the worst effects of Gavelkind were avoided.

The Domesday Book, which calls the county Chenth, gives us the first detailed account of how the land was populated and farmed. It was a manorial economy of a kind unique in England. The manors, of which about four hundred are listed, were given by the king to Canterbury's two great abbeys and to secular and ecclesiastical lords like Hugh de Montfort and Odo, Bishop of Bayeux, who had come over with the Conqueror, and their sub-tenants were natives with names like Adam or Wadard. The Domesday population has been estimated by Frank Jessup as sixty thousand, densest in the Folkestone hinterland and the neighbourhood of Maidstone. Eight boroughs are mentioned, Canterbury, Dover, Rochester, Faversham, Sandwich, Fordwich, Hythe and Romney, all of them, with the exception of Canterbury, a sea or river port, and all small. Canterbury had only two hundred and fifty houses, Rochester eighty-five. Sandwich was probably the largest, with a population of about two thousand. Kentishmen were, in the main, hamlet dwellers. Outside the Weald, still a thinly populated forest, almost every village which exists today was already established, and contemporary church records name another hundred and fifty not mentioned in Domesday. Each soon had its Norman church, of which the grandest is St Margaret's at Cliffe, a mile from the South Foreland, and one of the smallest and most enriched by sculpture and wall painting is in the village of Barfreston. The land was intensely cultivated. Kent never adopted the open-field system of the Midlands. The fields were grouped together much like a modern farm, enclosed against sheep and cattle by wattle fences. No houses of the period survive. None was built of stone. The wealthier people lived in modest timber halls, the poor in wattle-and-daub cabins roofed by thatch.

The exceptions were the castles. Kent is particularly rich in them. Eleven were built in the first two centuries after the Norman invasion, but only one, Dover, lies on the coast. The others, Saltwood, Canterbury, Chilham, Leeds, Sutton Valence, Allington, Rochester, Tonbridge, West Malling and Eynsford, were built by local lords to defend river crossings and keep the population under control. Rochester will be described later, and four of the others can stand as typical of the rest. *Saltwood* is hidden by trees at the edge of its village and cannot be visited, but from the air it looks magnificently feudal, as if it should not really belong in so green a pasturage. When Sir Kenneth Clark bought it in 1954, almost unseen, he found it 'one of the most enchanting spots imaginable: a high wall running round an oval lawn of about an acre, broken by various staircases and turrets, and the ruins of a banqueting hall and a chapel'. He made of the hall the most gothic of libraries, and filled the turret rooms with incomparable works of art. Saltwood had been the property of Archbishop Lanfranc soon after the Conquest, then of Hugh de Montfort at the time of Domesday, and the great gatehouse was added by another Archbishop, Courtenay, in 1390. Though moated and with all the apparatus of fortification, it can never have been defensible against determined attack, and remains a work of architectural pageantry, a fairytale castle when lit by the rising or setting sun.

*Tonbridge* castle is quite different. Although it lies just off the busiest street of the town, overlooking the adolescent Medway, the motorist might easily miss it, for the immediate approach is masked by trees and the huge earthen cone of the Norman motte, an achievement of almost Iron Age proportions. The keep which surmounted the motte has disappeared, and was replaced in 1300 by an entrance of two rotund drum towers squeezing between their cheeks a gateway closed by a portcullis. Around the whole bailey is a deep moat. It is formidable evidence of a conquering power determined to overawe the town, and cautions us against imagining

Kent in the early Middle Ages to have been a corner of England which knew neither fear nor cruelty.

The third castle, Norman in origin, is *Leeds*. Its setting is famous, standing in a moat so wide that it seems to be a lake and the castle an island, and surrounded on all sides by pasture that has gained in freshness by conversion into a golf course. The buildings form a Siamese twin castle, the oldest, slimmest part, the Gloriette, joined by a two-storey bridge to the 1822 reconstruction of the main block. Do not regret this date, for no more perfect image of feudal romanticism can be seen in England, and it matches perfectly the Gloriette annex of which the lower storeys are from the reign of Edward I, whose favourite castle this was. Inside, both parts have been modernized and furnished to the standard of the most splendid country houses, and are rented for small residential conferences to organizations which can afford it.

But of all the Norman foundations, *Dover Castle* is incomparably the greatest, and, with Canterbury Cathedral, Kent's pre-eminent monument. Its situation, for a start, is superbly dramatic, on the summit of steep hill above the town and harbour, a grey cliff surmounting a white cliff, a proclamation of suzerainty over the

27

whole island at its very portal, a tangible affirmation of the county's arrogant motto *Invicta*, and a symbol of continuity throughout our history.

There was a massive earthen fort here originally, and within its still visible ramparts the Romans built their lighthouse and the Saxons their greatest church, St Mary in Castro. The defences were elaborated in King Harold's day, and again by William the Conqueror immediately after Hastings. The great keep which dominates the complex was raised by Henry II in the 1160s within a curtain wall defended by seventeen towers, eight of which still bear the names of Norman knights. The keep is a prodigious building, ninety-five feet to the tops of the turrets and proportionately square. The walls are as much as twenty feet thick, hollowed at intervals to admit large chambers, and there are two main halls, two chapels, a well two hundred and fifty feet deep, and great internal staircases. It was not only a fortress of stupendous strength, but a residence of regal grandeur. Richard I stayed here, Henry V in triumph after Agincourt, Henry VIII before embarking for the Field of the Cloth of Gold. Here Charles I received his bride, Henrietta Maria, and here his son landed after his Restoration. Right up till

*Deal Castle is the most unaltered specimen of the fortifications built by Henry VIII along the southern and eastern shores of Britain. The present stone approach to the keep on the landward side is a replacement for the original drawbridge. Although the castle appears from this direction to have only one storey, it actually has five, which support a hedgehog of defence works guarding the anchorage of the Downs.*

the Second World War the castle and outworks were added to, altered, strengthened, its rooftops flattened to support artillery, and underground galleries, part medieval, part Napoleonic, were honeycombed into the hill. By 1990 the public will be admitted to the cavernous headquarters from which the evacuation of Dunkirk was directed, and Churchill watched the attack on Britain by air and sea and the gunfire from the French coast. A military garrison was stationed here as late as 1952, and now Dover Castle is in the care of English Heritage, a proper custodian and a proper name for the most historic castle in the land.

In the later Middle Ages there was no overall scheme for the defence of the coast. Reliance was placed on ships recruited from the Cinque Ports. The original five were Sandwich, Dover, Hythe, Romney and Hastings, to which were added the 'Ancient Towns' of Winchelsea and Rye, and later still, 'limbs' up to a total of thirty, including Deal, Ramsgate, Faversham, Folkestone, Margate, Lydd, Fordwich and Tenterden. Their duties were not onerous. Jointly they undertook to provide the king with a fleet of fifty-seven ships for fifteen days a year. In return they enjoyed certain privileges like freedom from central taxation, the right to raise tolls on passing merchant ships, and a claim on all wreckage flung on their shores. The ports (only one of which, Dover, remains a major harbour) are now invested in recollection with a sort of marine chivalry which their conduct did not justify. Their acts of piracy were overlooked, and a bitter rivalry existed between them and other English ports which sometimes led to open conflict. The end of their hegemony came with the founding by Henry VIII of a regular Navy, and the silting up of the river mouths on which the majority of the Cinque Ports stood. Today the only relic of their privileges is to carry the canopy over the monarch at coronations, and to appoint their Lord Warden, an honorary office held among others by Wellington, Pitt, Curzon, Churchill and today the Queen Mother. Walmer Castle is their official residence, and the Duke of Wellington died there, but most of his successors have found it too tourist-ridden and uncomfortable for their stay to be agreeable.

After the Reformation, when Henry VIII feared invasion by the Catholic kings of Continental Europe, he organized the first cohesive defence system since the Romans' Saxon Shore. Knowing that his new Navy was too small to patrol the Channel effectively, he constructed forts round the eastern and southern coasts from Essex to Cornwall. Four of them were in Kent – Sandown, Deal, Walmer and Sandgate – and with the existing defences of Dover and new fortifications built on the Thames and Medway estuaries, they formed a chain of forts along the most vulnerable part of the coast. Sandown, Deal and Walmer were closely grouped within a three-

mile span to protect the Downs, the favourite Fleet anchorage between the shore and the Goodwin Sands while they awaited a favourable wind to take them down-Channel.

Little remains of Sandown or Sandgate castles, but Deal and Walmer are still in perfect condition. *Deal* is the grandest and least altered. It is best seen from the air, for the ground view conceals its symmetrical design, like a Tudor rose: six circular platforms on which the guns were mounted, six smaller bastions below, all arranged round a low central tower. Inside, it retains its cavernous galleries and barracks, ingeniously planned both for easy egress by the garrison and puzzling access by an enemy, and although it looks from outside like a single storey, it has five levels, each with their gun ports. The whole is surrounded by a dry moat, once crossed by a drawbridge, now by one fixed. *Walmer* has been much more altered over the centuries, and its low profile, crouched against bombardment, has been spoiled by later changes and additions, but the castle consequently has merits which Deal lacks – staterooms, and a garden of nineteenth-century excellence, partly made by Lady Hester Stanhope. None of Henry's castles was attacked until the Civil War, but they served their purpose as a deterrent, and it was from their shelter that the fire ships set out to confound the Spanish

*Walmer Castle is Deal's twin and they lie little more than a mile apart. Built by Henry VIII to the same crouching formula, and heavily fortified on the seaward side, it has been much altered to provide a comfortable dwelling for the Lords Warden of the Cinque Ports, one of whom, Wellington, died at Walmer.*

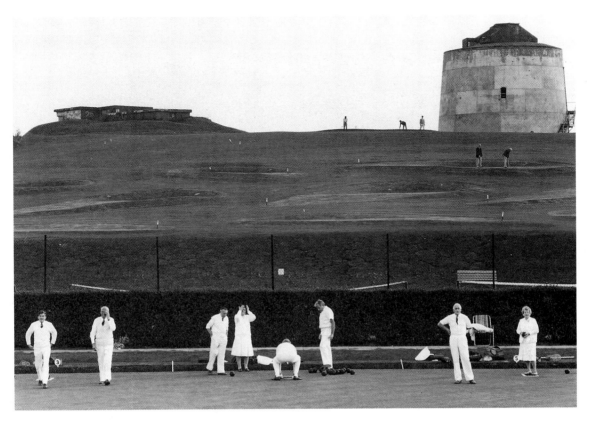

*The bowling green at Folkestone and, above it, the massive tambourine of the first martello tower to be built when Napoleon threatened invasion. Constructed primarily as emplacements for guns which were mounted on the roof, they were also big enough to serve as a barrack for a small garrison.*

Armada. In both world wars Deal and Walmer were again employed for offence and defence. Now they are museums.

In the Stuart and Georgian reigns strong defences were developed along Kent's northern coast, which will be described in the last chapter. The next major military works were made as a precaution against a Napoleonic invasion. From this period date the early fortification of the Western Heights at Dover, the barracks at Gillingham and Fort Clarence at Rochester, but the best known, paradoxically because they seem so puny, are the Martello towers and the Royal Military Canal. Some of the towers, of which there were originally seventy-four, stretching from Suffolk to the Solent, can still be seen at Hythe, Dymchurch and elsewhere, most converted into dwellings or storerooms. They were circular blockhouses with a gun-mounting on the roof and loopholes for muskets below, and accommodation for twenty-two soldiers inside. They were never tested by assault, perhaps fortunately, because although they were constructed very solidly, their weakness was their exposure to mortar fire lobbed vertically onto the gun platforms. William Cobbett thought them 'ridiculous things', costing millions. But he reserved his greatest scorn for the Military Canal, constructed between 1804 and 1807 from Hythe to Rye as the northern

defence of Romney Marsh. 'To keep out the French!' wrote Cobbett. 'Those armies which had so often crossed the Rhine and the Danube were to be kept back by a canal, thirty-feet wide at the most!' The enormous labour involved was scarcely worthwhile, for although the canal was twenty-three miles long, carefully engineered, with knee-bends at intervals of a musket shot to stagger an assault, if it had been pierced at a single point, say near Hythe, the rest would have been useless, exposing to rearward attack the thousands of men needed to man it. But it had other uses, as a canal for barges, and to drain the unsalubrious marshes. Trafalgar made it redundant. Today it is an historical curiosity and a scenic attraction, especially the stretch below Appledore, and affords great pleasure to fishermen and canoeists.

In Victorian times important new works were carried out in the estuaries, but the most elaborate of all were the extensions of the Western Heights defences at Dover, excavated in the chalk to create moats, tunnels and redoubts, a complex series of underground barracks large enough to hold a substantial part of the British

*The Royal Military Canal was twenty-three miles long, stretching in an arc from Hythe to Rye. Below Appledore the waterway is overlooked by a pill-box of the Second World War, when the canal was once again put to tactical use, although it was originally dug as a defensive moat during the Napoleonic Wars to seal off the northern rim of Romney Marsh where the French were likely to attempt a landing.*

Army. The most ingenious feature of all was the Grand Shaft, two spiral staircases wound round each other, by which the fortifications could be reached from the town. Built at colossal expense, they were never needed for their intended use.

To complete the story of Kent as the nation's bastion, its role as sword and shield, one must sketch briefly its part in both world wars. No fortifications were built on the same scale as in previous centuries. In 1914 the Navy took over the main defensive task, notably the famous Dover Patrol of drifters and trawlers, supplemented by cordons of nets and mines, which protected the flanks of the strait from German submarines and destroyers. Over five million men were ferried to Calais and Boulogne without a single casualty. In the Second World War, Kent became not so much a sea base as an armed camp. If Hitler had carried out his invasion, *Sealion*, the initial assault would have come not on north-east Kent but on the stretch of coast running from Folkestone westwards as far as Brighton, with a gap at Beachy Head. The *Schwerpunkt* was to be between Hythe and Dymchurch. Parachutists would drop on the Downs behind Folkestone, and the force would swing inland to capture Dover from the rear, and then carve a wide bridgehead through Ashford and Hawkhurst. Here they would link up with the divisions from Brighton, and push forward to capture crossings over the Thames west of London. Against this threat the British ground defences were at first pitiably thin. After Dunkirk only eight divisions were available to guard four hundred miles of the eastern and southern coastline, with ten more in reserve, all inadequately equipped. In the vital sector between Sheppey and Rye there was only one division, at half strength, armed with twenty-three field guns and no armoured vehicles at all. Defences were hurriedly improvised. The beaches, fields and lanes were mined and obstructed, the Martello towers mounted with machine guns, the Royal Military Canal refortified, and brick pillboxes erected far inland, of which some can still be seen in the meadows, like that at Bodiam Castle just over the Sussex border, where it sits incongruously under the shadow of the great stone fortress built in the fourteenth century for the same purpose.

But there was nothing in Kent faintly comparable to the Germans' Atlantic Wall or the monster concrete fortifications of the Channel Islands. If the beaches were overrun, successive stop-lines would be held as far as the outer defence of London. This ran along the ridge of the Downs north of Maidstone and Sevenoaks, and can be seen rising prominently ahead of the motorist driving on the A21 towards the capital. When General Montgomery took over the Kentish sector early in 1941, with his headquarters at Tunbridge Wells, he thinned out the coastal battalions to create mobile

33

reserves, and fortified four towns, Dover, Folkestone, Ashford and Canterbury, as strong points to be held to the last. The whole of eastern Kent became a theatre for manoeuvre on a mounting scale.

But ultimately the survival of the nation depended upon the Navy and Air Force. Never in its history had Kent become involved in so great or protracted a battle. When the fighter aircraft had successfully defended south-east England, their duty was to protect Channel and Thames shipping, then absorb the shock of the pilotless rockets, and finally support the Allied invasion of Europe. After Dunkirk, as the official history of the RAF puts it, 'the world's largest airforce was within an hour's flight of the world's largest target', and Kent lay between them. In August 1940, when the Battle of Britain began in earnest, the main fighter bases were at Manston (Thanet), Biggin Hill, West Malling, Lympne, Eastchurch, Hawkinge and Detling, and each of them was repeatedly, though temporarily, put out of action by German bombs, as were many of the coastal radar stations. On the afternoon of 15 August, the turning point of the battle, over seventeen hundred enemy aircraft crossed the coast, four hundred of them between Dover and Dungeness, and seventy-four were shot down. All Kent watched these battles from harvest fields and village streets, knowing instinctively that failure would be followed by invasion. The Hurricanes and Spitfires (of which one is preserved in a glass museum at Manston) became their symbols and the pilots instant heroes. So much greater was the loss of aircraft than their replacement from the factories that if the Germans had sustained their attacks on the Kentish airfields for three more weeks, our fighter reserves would have been exhausted. But in September Goering overflew Kent to concentrate his attack on London.

The ring of defences round the coast, developed over a period of two thousand years and increasing in sophistication, can scarcely be said to make much impact on the present scene. The airfields are as peaceful as the Iron Age fort at Bigbury. Canterbury's Roman-medieval walls do little more than protect the inner city from its hectic circuit road, and Henry VIII's castles are but features in ornamental parks. Here and there you will see, behind prohibitive wire and notices, metallic structures of secret purpose that hint at the county's continuing defensive role.

In the main, Kent's seacoast is a chain of resort and holiday towns, enlivened by its ports. Little of it is free from building, and only the chalk cliffs give it a memorable scenic character, mostly from the seaward side. Round the knuckle of Thanet extend Birchington, Westgate, Margate and Ramsgate, with prettier Broadstairs squeezed between the last two. They are old fishing

Above: Broadstairs, with its
attractive streets, scalloped bay
and Regency-type houses, has
always enjoyed a more intimate
character than its two larger
neighbours, Margate and
Ramsgate.

Right: Designed by the
comparatively unknown
architect Henry Hemsley in
1824, St George's, Ramsgate,
has one of the finest interiors of
early nineteenth-century
churches. Among its most
attractive features are the
galleries on either side of the
nave.

*Above: During the annual Dickens Festival at Broadstairs bathers dress the part. Charles Dickens was a frequent visitor here, completing* David Copperfield *in what is now misleadingly called Bleak House, and* Nicholas Nickleby *at the Royal Albion Hotel.*

*Left: Margate, at the height of its summer season. It was the first town in England to become popular as a sea-bathing resort. As early as the 1730s all classes of Londoners were flocking to Margate by river-boat and, with the coming of the railway in 1846, the once-decaying fishing village expanded enormously.*

villages developed as holiday resorts with crowded beaches, and sprawl into Thanet in widening circles or outwards towards the North Foreland in fancy crescents of neat houses for the retired. There is a vivacity about these towns in summertime, as there has always been since Margate became Londoners' favourite resort in the reign of George III, when a local man invented the bathing machine. Margate's scimitar seafront, with its miniature harbour, does credit to the planners who have kept commercialism under control. It also has one of the stateliest railway stations in the country. Ramsgate is grander but shoddier, its tiered terraces and crescents above the harbour suggesting a Regency elegance which it has lost.

In all these towns except Broadstairs, which is charming in its small-scale inconsequence, as Dickens found, the main blemish is the ugliness of Victorian public and private building, proof of their unsuccessful search for an architectural style that would match their vigour and inventiveness. Hence the proliferation of bow-windows, encrusted turrets, ornament illogically slapped on, and

the shapelessness of the town plans away from the shore. The Thanet coastal resorts have recently lost popularity by failing to respond adequately to the competition of the Mediterranean. Margate, it is true, has its amusement park, and Ramsgate has developed fast as a port. But much of the holiday accommodation is in terraced houses with shared bathrooms and poor facilities, and a great deal needs to be done by building modern hotels, marinas and other leisure attractions to arrest the decline.

Deal is better, for its High Street and the alleys which join it to the seafront, and because it has never been over-popular as a resort, remaining, as John Newman writes, 'a fascinating dense texture, a late seventeenth-century town, unlike anything in England'. But the real jewel of the coast is Sandwich, the most attractive town in Kent. Within its ancient ramparts, which you can still patrol, the streets are narrow and tightly packed, lined by little houses, many of them medieval or Tudor, and supplemented or replaced over the centuries by others that never violate the pattern or the scale. One of the most recent and loveliest is The Salutation, designed by Lutyens in his best Queen Anne style, standing alone in a Gertrude Jekyll garden. Three ancient churches rise over the russet roofs, and the entrance to the town is by a Tudor barbican gate. Yet Sandwich is not too perfect. Its busy town life removes the suspicion that it may be over-consciously picturesque. One flaw is the river. Here the Stour is tidal and the mud flats at low tide are unpleasing to walk beside and useless for any craft except small pleasure boats. Yet the river mouth was the reason why Sandwich was designated one of the original Cinque Ports and became so prosperous. Its harbour silted up in the sixteenth century, and when Defoe passed this way in 1720, he found it 'an old, decayed, poor, miserable town', and Cobbett a century later, 'as villainous a hole as one could wish to see, surrounded by some of the finest land in the world'. The land, apart from its famous golf courses, now seems less than fine, cluttered by garages and industrial buildings, but the town is so lovely that one can scarcely imagine it to have been anything else. Perhaps Defoe and Cobbett were thinking of the comforts it offered, then inadequate, now irreproachable.

So to Dover. The callipers of the curving jetties enclose two harbours separated by a beach, and the town occupies the valley of a little river, now running partly underground. There are many excellent things in Dover apart from its castle, like its fourteenth-century Maison Dieu and the row of Regency houses under the cliff by the ferry terminal. Much of the town was rebuilt after terrible damage suffered by bombardment in the Second World War, and it is now not only the busiest port in Britain, but its evident prosperity is a national advertisement. Folkestone bustles less and is out-

*The russet roofs of Sandwich from one of its church towers. Still the most delightful small town in Kent, it was once a leading Cinque Port. Although it has lost its importance as a harbour, it retains its medieval street pattern and combines a decent regard for its architectural legacy with the bustling activity of a modern market town.*

wardly more attractive, at least on its cliff side, where the smart hotels and boarding houses of the Leas overlook the sea. There is a tiny medieval village buried in the centre, with one good church, and it has a splendid high-stepping railway viaduct and a monstrous public library of 1880. Folkestone is in fact almost entirely a creation of the nineteenth century, when the railway made it fashionable and the port became a poor relation of Dover's.

What concerns Folkestone people most, and in diminishing circles of anxiety the whole of Kent, is the prospect of the Channel Tunnel, which will submerge just north of the town and, they fear, destroy its serenity and the commerce of the port. The works had scarcely begun when this book was written, and will not be completed before 1993. As it is the biggest strategical project in the history of

*The Warren lies immediately east of Folkestone. It is a strange, tumbled strip of coastline, formed by the slipping of the chalk cliff, which has exposed a wealth of fossils, and is a natural bed for rare plants and wild life.*

40

the county, the purpose, plan and likely impact of the tunnel is worth examining.

The preliminary arguments have been exhaustive, stretching backwards for nearly two centuries. In 1803 a candle-lit tunnel for horse-drawn traffic was suggested, ludicrously, to Napoleon as a means of invading Britain, and he gave it scant attention before rejecting it. In 1848 the French produced a plan for a floating tube. In the 1880s a tunnel was actually begun from each coast, then abandoned by the British for fear that a few hundred Frenchmen, presumably in disguise, might sieze the Kentish terminal for long enough to allow an army to invade. The Navy would be underpassed. The promoters argued that the tunnel could be shattered by remote control, drowning the invaders more effectively than the Pharaoh's army in the Red Sea, or filled with carbon dioxide, but public opinion sided with the military, and the two aborted tunnels, each about a mile long, were left desolate. In the 1960s a further attempt was again halted, more for environmental and financial reasons than military. In the 1980s the tunnel idea was revived and seems at last to be approaching fulfilment.

The objections to the principle of any fixed link with the Continent continue. There is a deep-rooted regret that Britannia will no longer be *intacta*. The tunnel will be a gigantic French rape. Our history, and the theme that throbs through much of our literature, is pride in our insularity. The Channel is a moat not only defensively, but psychologically. It defines the limits of our culture in a way that no river or mountain barrier between states can equal. It is as divisive as an ocean, and to bridge it, even submarinely, is to lose something of our national virtue. These fears, seldom explicitly stated, underlie opposition on more practical grounds. The tunnel will expose us to every Continental ill. Vermin will cross dryshod, bringing rabies. Terrorists will load vehicles with deadly charges timed to explode in mid-passage. Accidents to chemical loads will create equal hazards. A handful of malcontent strikers at either end will find it easy to interrupt traffic for days on end. Passengers in so long a tunnel will panic from claustrophobia or be stifled by fumes. And what if a train catches fire? It is argued, for profounder reasons, that the whole venture is an error on a monstrous scale. Dover will become a ghost town, its working population deprived of their main function. Trade and industry will be sucked to the south-east of England, impoverishing the Midlands and the north. Kent will become a marshalling yard, its orchards and valleys sacrificed to warehousing, road and rail sidings, factories, and an enormous surge in population. Its roads will be choked by juggernauts of an ever-increasing size. If these disasters are avoided by restrictive planning, the French will welcome the development that Kent rejects, since north-west France is poorer and quite different in character from south-east England. Xenophobia surfaces. The whole project is a deep-seated French plot to drain away our substance and fill our shops with Continental goods.

The replies to all this are equally cogent. There are technical ways round all the anticipated dangers. We should take pride in the greatest engineering achievement of this century, costing £4.6 billion, privately financed, and symbolic of Britain's acceptance of a European role. The benefits, both of construction and use, will spread to every part of the country, and far from clogging Kent's roads with traffic and its fields with commercial buildings, the tunnel will actually lighten the burden, since loaded trains from the north will run straight through to western Europe. 'An urgent sales order from Holland,' runs the Eurotunnel blurb, 'leaves a depot in Cardiff at 5 a.m. It will be delivered in Amsterdam before the close of business. Students returning from Switzerland board the overnight sleeper in Basle. They'll be back in Edinburgh in time for afternoon lessons.'

The present ferries cannot guarantee so fast, convenient and all-weather a route, but they will not be eliminated by the tunnel. Cross-Channel traffic is expected to double before the end of the century, and tunnel and ferries will compete for custom. Many tourists will prefer the sea passage, from habit and for the drama of it, risking sickness and fog, and long-distance marine traffic will continue to use the Channel ports. A considerable range of vehicles, which for size or safety reasons cannot use the tunnel will remain loyal to the sea routes. Meanwhile, claims the pro-tunnel lobby, the construction will create some fifty thousand jobs, and five thousand permanently in the south-east alone. Once it is built, insular prejudices will be cured by using it, and like the Forth Bridge a century ago it will become an object of wonder and a feat for self-congratulation.

There will be not one but three tunnels, two of them seven metres in diameter for rail traffic, and a central, smaller tunnel for servicing, ventilation, access and emergencies, joined to the main tunnels by cross-passages at frequent intervals. They will be bored through the chalk marl, a substratum as easily sliced as cheese but impervious to water, forty metres below the sea bed. All vehicles will be carried by trains drawn by electric locomotives, running at ten-minute intervals at peak times and every half-hour throughout the night, between terminals at Cheriton, north of Folkestone, and Sangatte near Calais. No pre-booking will be necessary. The journey will be thirty-one miles, twenty-four of them under the sea, taking about thirty-five minutes, an hour faster than the fastest ferry. The Cheriton terminal will be squeezed between the Downs

*Sugarloaf Hill, north of Folkestone, from its neighbour, Castle Hill. The Channel Tunnel will begin its thirty-one-mile journey (twenty-four of them under water) by burrowing through each of these hills in turn.*

and the M20, shuttle-shaped for shuttle trains, obnoxious only to its immediate neighbours, but for its users, so the promoters claim, a miracle of efficiency and delight. In transit, passengers will be able to leave their cars to walk around them within the confines of the carriage, admiring posters, drinking Coke. It will be a 100-mph cocoon, shooting from daylight to daylight, and the interval unalarmingly submarine. For those without cars or lorries there will be direct passenger services from London to Paris and Brussels, the whole journey taking three hours, city centre to city centre, which compares very favourably even with air travel.

These are the current arguments on each side. It remains to be seen which will prevail.

# 2

# *The Weald*

THE WEALD, WHICH for outsiders is the typical, the ideal Kent, a district of small villages, few towns, many farms, woods, oast houses and fruit blossom, has given to the whole county the name 'the Garden of England' which properly belongs to it alone. So closely is it identified with Kent, its very heartland, that it is often overlooked that the Weald extends over a much greater part of Sussex, and even spreads into Surrey and Hampshire. The word derives from the Anglo-Saxon *wald*, a forest, which in the sixteenth century was sometimes corrupted into 'wild', and some authorities trace the name even further back to Andredsweald, a Jutish version of Anderida, the Roman fort at Pevensey. What is certain is that it designated the tract of thick woodland that from primeval times filled the basin between the North and South Downs. Its exact boundaries have long been in dispute, and have never needed formal definition, since the Weald is more a scenic than a legal or administrative term. For the present purpose let us say that the forest once extended over a hundred miles from Lympne to near Winchester, at its broadest in Kent, stretching for thirty miles from the greensand ridge to Romney Marsh, and divided equally between the Low Weald (also called the Vale) and the High Weald. The Downs were not part of it. Tonbridge and Tunbridge Wells lay within it, but not Sevenoaks; Cranbrook and Tenterden, but neither Ashford nor Maidstone.

When one speaks of a forest, it should not imply an impenetrable or totally uninhabited jungle. Traces of Neolithic man have been found in it. It did form, however, a sufficient obstacle for Caesar to skirt it, and though Harold marched through the Weald to fight and die at Battle, William the Conqueror sensibly took the long way round through Dover to reach London. One must imagine it as a forest chiefly of oak and beech, with much fallen timber and an undergrowth of bramble and holly, which occasionally opened into glades, as at Cranbrook and Brenchley. At the stream crossings and in the Vale it would have been very marshy. To this day the people of the ridges say that Weald men must have speckled bellies and

*Previous page: Here, near Horsmonden, is a typical Wealden scene: two oast houses stand to the right of a group of farm buildings and cottages; there is an orchard in the foreground, and cornlands are interspersed with root crops. A small wood or 'shaw' stands against the skyline.*

*Above right: The Weald of Kent, seen from the slopes of the North Downs near Wrotham. Between the chalk Downs and the greensand ridge on the horizon extends a broad valley. The rivers Darent and Medway cut northwards through both barriers to meet the Thames at its estuary.*

*Below right: The Downs, here open and sheep-grazed but often wooded and cultivated, look southward over the Weald. From a distance, it can appear almost as thickly forested as it was before the medieval clearances.*

46

*Contrasting foliage outside a cottage near Penshurst.*

webbed feet. There were deer wandering freely in it, and wild pig.

So long as the population of Kent was small enough, about ten thousand, there was ample space for farming on the deforested land north and east of the Weald and they had no incentive to explore the wilderness. The Romans drove one major road through it south from Rochester to Hastings, and a single villa, north of Benenden, has been excavated on its route, but the proper penetration of the Weald began only after they had abandoned Britain.

It was at first simply a matter of fattening domestic swine on acorns and beech mast for a couple of months in early autumn, a 'pannage' which was unorganized and implied no settlement or right of tenure, but gradually during the Anglo-Saxon period huts were erected in favourite spots, open spaces enclosed by rough fences, and some were given outlandish names like Estercogheringdenne (Ashenden) or Tenetwarabrocas (Tenderden). The termination '-den', frequent in village and farm names today, signified a clearing in the wood, '-hurst' a wooded knoll, '-ham' a small

*The land has been so thickly
settled between the surviving
woods in the High Weald that it
is difficult to find any place from
which at least two farmsteads
are not visible. The country,
alternating between orchard,
meadow and arable land,
remains as rural as it was three
centuries ago.*

homestead, '-ley' a meadow; and proper names were added to
them, like Biddenden (Bidda's clearing), Penshurst (Pen's wood) or
Angley (land that belonged to the Angles).

These hog pastures were the origins of the present villages. It was
during the sixth, seventh and eighth centuries that they came to be
occupied more permanently, and the manors lying outside the
Weald obtained title to certain of them. In 791, for instance, Offa
granted pannage at Sandhurst to the monks of Canterbury,
Tenterden was the 'den' of the men of Thanet, and Chilmington in
Great Chart parish was owned by the manor of Reculver. In his
book *The Jutish Forest*, K.P.Witney has ingeniously traced the
routes by which the pigs were driven from the manors to the forest.
The herdsmen converged on it from the east, north-east and north
by winding tracks that avoided natural obstacles and became the
basis of today's network of lanes. It was only in the nineteenth
century that a much-needed transverse road across the tracks was
laid down between Biddenden, Headcorn and Sutton Valence, and

49

to this day there is no direct road east-west through the Vale parallel to the railway, as anyone will have discovered if he misses a train at Pluckley and tries to catch it at Paddock Wood.

By the time of Domesday there were some fifty 'dens' in the Weald, but only Benenden and Newenden were substantial enough for the surveyors to record them. Many others which are known to have existed, like Tonbridge, were omitted entirely. In the early 1200s, says Mr Witney, the ecclesiastical records mention every medieval parish church except Capel, and though most were originally of timber, relics of Norman architecture survive here and there, like the famous door of Staplehurst's church with its Viking-like iron scrolls. The holdings quickly multiplied, subdivided by the law of Gavelkind, and arable began to encroach on the pannage. The forest was gnawed away from within by arduous felling of the trees, not by fire, since only the pine is combustible as it stands. It was a remarkably rapid transformation, comparable to the American settlement of the forests east of the Mississippi. By the mid-fourteenth century the Weald must have gained much of its present

*The church at Horsmonden stands a mile away from its village with only a large farm as its neighbour, and sheep wander freely into its churchyard.*

50

The village street of Biddenden curves slightly towards its church; the pavements are of Bethersden 'marble' – limestone encrusted with mollusc shells. The plasterwork, timber-framing and many of the casement windows are original, dating from the sixteenth century.

appearance, cultivated and hedged, leaving small woods or 'shaws' as reminders of what had been achieved.

At the same time iron mining was revived. The Romans had mined in the Weald, but not the Jutes. The iron ore was found twenty feet deep in the clay as round nuggets, and it was excavated by bell-pits which widened at the bottom. The ore was then smelted out of the stone in a blast furnace or bloomery, operated by a water wheel which worked both the bellows and the heavy hammer which shaped the ore into ingots. The 'hammer ponds', sometimes a chain of them, made by damming streams at intervals, provided a sufficient head of water to turn the wheel, and fuel for the furnaces came plentifully from the surrounding woodland. When a wide area of trees had been felled, the bloomery was abandoned for another site deeper in the forest. There were never very many of them, and their presence was always inconspicuous. A document of 1573 records only eight furnaces and six forges in the Kentish Weald, near such villages as Biddenden, Tenterden, Goudhurst, Lamberhurst and Cowden, and their products were much in

demand for cannon, firebacks, tools, ornamental ironwork (the railings round St Paul's Cathedral came from Lamberhurst) and even iron grave slabs.

The rise of the iron industry coincided with woollen manufacture on a scale that rapidly increased when Edward III invited Flemish weavers to settle in Kent. It was confined to a small area round Cranbrook, Goudhurst and Hawkhurst, and for four centuries, until the eighteenth, they produced England's finest broadcloth. The Flemings introduced the technique of ridding the wool of grease by working fuller's earth – a naturally absorbent clay – into the cloth, and pounding it with wooden hammers, powered by another set of water wheels. The weaving was done on hand looms set up in cottages and hall houses, and later in cloth halls for a number of weavers. The cloth was carried out of the Weald on ponies, much of it for export from Sandwich.

The two industries in combination made of the Weald the chief manufacturing district of Britain, and a scene of activity which is difficult to reconcile with its wholly rural appearance today. Camden wrote of the hammers, 'which fill the neighbourhood, night and day, with continuous noise', and of the glare of furnaces

*Until the mid-eighteenth century the Weald was one of the most famous sheep-rearing areas of England, and woollen cloth was its chief manufacture for some four hundred years. The sheep, but not the industry, survive on a much reduced scale, and flocks like this occasionally block the lanes. Sheep-dipping is carried on in greater privacy.*

lighting the night sky. Just in time to avoid the excesses of the Industrial Revolution, the iron industry moved to the Midlands where coal, a better fuel than charcoal, lay in proximity to iron ore, and the more homely methods of weaving Kentish cloth failed to stand the competition of the Scottish and Cotswold mills. There are relics of this long phase in place names like Hammer Mill, in decaying brickwork astride a stream, and the many small ponds from which fuller's earth was dug. But its chief legacy is architectural.

No other part of the country can show a greater wealth of late-medieval and Tudor buildings. The churches, it is true, cannot rival East Anglia's, nor the public buildings a town hall like King's Lynn, for Kentish ragstone was poor material for cutting and weathering. But at the turn of almost every Wealden lane there survives a cottage or a manor house built by a prosperous weaver or ironmaster. The materials are wood, brick, plaster, tile and glass, all indigenous, the humbler dwellings often weather-boarded or tile-hung for greater warmth in winter, and the roofs descending almost to the ground in a 'cat slide'. As so much timber was available locally, the larger houses were framed by huge beams of oak or chestnut (the greatest that survives is the roof of Penshurst's

*A sixteenth-century cloth hall in Smarden – one of the centres of the former cloth-making industry, which left behind a wealth of manor houses and timbered buildings. A hoist for bales of wool stands beneath the gable, and two loft doors lead to the one-time spinning and storage rooms.*

*The earliest parts of Ightham Mote, now a National Trust property, date from the middle of the fourteenth century. Arranged four-square within the moat, and around an interior courtyard, the buildings form the ideal – if somewhat grand-scale – medieval Wealden manor house.*

medieval hall), which over the centuries have settled a little crookedly to natural angles of repose. A house like Castweazel, near Biddenden, or Old Wilsley, outside Cranbrook, medium-sized manor houses with capacious living rooms and bedrooms, illustrate their soundness and luxury. Ightham Mote, north of Hildenborough, is an example of a house built by a grander family on a grander scale, a moated manor of stone and timber round an open courtyard, lying low in its deep valley, and containing its original hall and two chapels, one fourteenth-century, the other Tudor. The house has been in continuous occupation and constantly modernized, but this is true of all Wealden houses, not to their disadvantage. Almost every hall house, like Pattenden near Goudhurst, has had a floor inserted to form a second storey above the hall, the blackened beams in the attic a reminder of how once the smoke coiled upwards from the centre of the hall's floor. These houses are found not only in the open country but in the main streets of towns like Tenterden, villages like Headcorn, Lenham and Smarden, lying companionably alongside their brick successors, and blending architectural tradition with innovation which was only abused in the Victorian age, as by the inn in the centre of Brenchley.

*Above: Built as a parsonage, this lovely sixteenth-century house stands outside the churchyard at Headcorn. It is a typical Wealden house, its great hall lit by a double-storeyed window, and the solar and other rooms jettied out front and back.*

*Left: Tenterden, one of the larger Wealden towns, contains nearly two hundred listed buildings. They are to be found along the main street and around the village-type green.*

*Opposite: Cranbrook is a typical Wealden town. Its houses form an exhibition of different building styles from the fifteenth century onwards, but its most prominent monument, apart from the church, is the nineteenth-century smock-mill.*

Tonbridge and Tunbridge Wells are in the Weald, but not of it. The only truly Wealden towns are Edenbridge, Tenterden and Cranbrook. The first preserves some good open-timber houses, but the other two are the jewels. Both have benefited greatly from their industrial past, and both have magnificent churches which bear witness to the generosity of the men who made money there. Tenterden's wide street has been called the most celebrated in Kent. It was the ancient market-place with ample room for stalls and cattle pens, and is now green with grass and trees, the low houses set back on each side to create a memorably beautiful townscape. No less than a hundred and eighty buildings in this small place have been listed as possessing architectural or historical merit; the most recent addition is the restored small stretch of abandoned railway leading towards the marshes. Cranbrook's centre is quite different, the main street turning a sudden right angle at the church, and Kent's most splendid windmill dominating the whole. The High Street climbs a gentle hill, flanked by contiguous shops and houses, more altered than Tenterden's and varied by every building style of the last four hundred years, original or mocked, to form an attractive double façade of great liveliness. At one end of the town is its well-known school, a pre-Elizabethan foundation, and at the other, Goddard's Green, a splendid half-timbered house with graceful gables added later.

But it is less the towns that create most people's image of the Weald than its villages and countryside, its 'wooded, dim, blue goodness'. Nowhere in England is the presence of man less objectionable. Many of the villages are set round greens, like Groombridge, Sandhurst, Horsmonden, Matfield (to my mind the prettiest of them all) or Benenden, with its famous cricket ground. Some straggle like Staplehurst along its Roman road, or throw out arms in many directions like Hawkhurst, or they lie in a valley dip like Lamberhurst, or climb a hill, like Charing, Pluckley and Goudhurst. All have preserved a cluster of cottages which unmistakeably identify the original village centre, and in some of them farm buildings crowd the church, like Lenham's great barn or the oast houses at Horsmonden. Their variety is created by the accidents of history or topography, the presence of some great house on the outskirts, or an encircling stream, and most were unplanned except for convenience, opening their few streets to unexpected views of houses set at awkward but pleasing angles (Marden and Smarden are good examples), unless a deliberate effort was made, as in Biddenden and Appledore, to approach the church by a short straight road flanked by houses of timber, brick and tile, or Chiddingstone, the most photographed of all, where a single row of houses faces the church.

*Matfield must count among Kent's loveliest villages. Around its duckpond and village green a series of large brick houses and integrated cottages – cherry-red and façaded by slender trees – are arranged at companionable intervals.*

There are many others, but they never seem too closely spaced, and the more hidden of them may be grateful for not being mentioned here, since they arose from, and still demand, seclusion. Not many have been spoiled by modern accretions, as control has been tight, and if there is an unsightly minority, it is because their development pre-dated the planning Acts or they lie on a main road, like Pembury (which has long deserved its new bypass) or Paddock Wood, which has suffered scenically but gained economically by becoming a commuters' haven and a Eurocentre transport depot.

The Low Weald is crossed by the River Beult which enters the

*Above: Lenham – a perfect village – is composed, unusually, of several interconnecting squares. Next to the church is a magnificent tithe barn.*

*Left: Chiddingstone from its churchyard. This tiny village is scarcely more than a row of sixteenth- and seventeenth-century houses and is more photographed than any other in Kent. The whole village is now owned by the National Trust.*

*Opposite: Although Elham lies on the eastern extremity of the Weald, it represents the homogeneity of colour in Wealden villages – the white and muted reds set against the surrounding green farmland.*

60

Left: Yalding is a large village situated near the junction of the rivers Beult and Medway. Manor house stands beside cottage, all combining the traditional materials of brick and tile, some faced with overlapping boarding to give them additional protection.

Above: an arable scene near Sandhurst, young wheat growing up a sweeping hill to a line of trees on the horizon.

Right: Great cylindrical bales of straw are rolled by modern balers after the combine harvester has done its work and, form unexpectedly sculptural patterns in the harvest fields.

Medway just beyond Yalding, and is bounded to the north by the greensand ridge. The High Weald is composed of low hills stretching towards Romney Marsh and Sussex, and has been designated, to the slight embarrassment of its inhabitants, An Area of Outstanding Natural Beauty. Apart from the configuration of the ground, the two Wealds do not differ much in character. Both are ideally rural. From where I write these words I look from the very edge of the High Weald across the Vale to the ridge which hides Canterbury. The view is one of changing fertility, slashed in spring by yellow fields of rape, golden with summer corn, or browned by autumn ploughing. The fields have kept their hedges, and so frequent are the intervening spinneys and hedgerow trees that you might think the country heavily wooded until you see it from the air, when the intensity of its cultivation is obvious. The farms are small in acreage and frequent, but the buildings so hug the ground or hide between spinneys, that in summer I can see from here

*A hop garden near Horsmonden (never call it a hop field!). Here the hops are beginning to grow; the 'bines' grow up strings suspended from an overhead cage of wire.*

64

In late August the harvest is about to begin: the bines will be pulled from the wires and the cones plucked from them by machinery, although until the Second World War this was always done by hand. The hops are taken straight from the hop garden, stripped from the bines, and loaded into the oast kiln, where they dry for about twenty-four hours.

scarcely one of them in the eight-mile Vale, and none that did not exist three hundred years ago.

There are fewer orchards now than then, and fewer hop gardens, but it is the hop that has given this part of Kent its special crop and a unique building, the oast house, whose white cowls speckle the landscape like highlights in a painting. The hop was probably introduced to England by the Flemings and was at first a cottage crop, frowned on as a drug, and was grown up poles. Today it winds clockwise up strings fixed to an overhead gantry of wire, and when fully grown forms aisles of pendulous yellow-green cones. In early September they are cut from the wire and the cones stripped from the bine. Until the Second World War this was always done by hand, by family teams from London's East End, and the invention of the hop-picking machine came just in time to replace their labour when they came to prefer, and could afford, less arduous holidays. The machine is a marvel to watch in operation, fingering the delicate cones and separating them from the bines and leaves.

*The largest group of oast houses in Kent is at Beltring, where Whitbread's assembled twenty of them. In constant use until a few years ago, modern technology has superseded them, but they have been retained to demonstrate past methods of hop-drying.*

*Poles stacked for erection as supports for the gantries of wire in the hop gardens. The poles have been a major product of the Wealden woods, which are often 'coppiced' to grow standard lengths of hazel or chestnut, creating stumps which can sprout ten feet of new growth in a single season.*

The oast house is basically a kiln or oven where the hops are dried. They are piled two feet deep on sacking laid over wooden slats on the first floor of the oast, and anthracite fires, until 1980 mixed with sulphur, are kept burning at ground level for as long as the harvest lasts. The heat rises through the hops, and the fumes (or 'reek') escape through the cowls, which act like chimneys at the top and revolve with the change of wind direction to maintain the proper draught. Their distinctive shape, open slanting hoods always painted white, was evolved by long experiment, but the oast house in its most familiar form dates only from the late eighteenth century, when it was built square in brick and sometimes stone with pyramidal roofs, and in the nineteenth-century round. The two shapes are often seen in proximity, usually two or three kilns to each farmyard, but sometimes massed in long rows, like the most famous of them, the Whitbread group at Beltring, where no fewer than twenty stand like soldiers, their white doors punctuating the parade at ground level to match the cowls sailing against the skyline.

Modern technology is rapidly making the oast house redundant. Duller sheds, fired by oil-burners and with squat chimneys, are replacing them all over the county. The old oasts, however, survive as storerooms for fruit and vegetables, or are converted into houses, usually preserving their cowls for scenic effect. Much ingenuity is displayed in these conversions, for the round kilns are awkward shapes to adapt for domestic use (imagine hanging a picture on the inside of a cone), and their classic outlines can be spoiled by the insertion of dormer windows. The attached cooling rooms where

*In the winter the apple orchards are bleakly desolate, but flower in spring and fruit in autumn, giving this part of Kent a colour that varies attractively throughout the year.*

the dried hops were laid ready for packing for the brewers are more easily made habitable. Excellent examples can be seen at Yalding (the Parsonage Oast) and at East Peckham.

Kent's hop gardens are mainly located in the Weald in the triangle formed by Maidstone, Tenterden and Tonbridge, but others are strung between Sittingbourne and Canterbury. The best are found in the valley of the Medway which Cobbett described as 'the very finest in the world', not just for its hop gardens but for its orchards of apples, pears, plums, cherries and filberts, and it remains today the loveliest stretch of countryside in Kent, with villages like Yalding, Wateringbury, Teston and East Farleigh, medieval stone bridges that span the river at intervals, and country houses like Mereworth, Nettlestead Place and Barham Court which add a Poussinesque effect to this most English of scenes.

The woodland of the Weald is extensive but seldom covers large areas, apart from the Forestry Commission's Hemsted or Bedgebury. As early as the sixteenth century William Lambarde could write, 'The Weald is now (thanked be God) wholly replenished with people'. It is remarkable that so many woods are left at all. They were cut for fuel and as beams for buildings, or cleared for agriculture, and Henry VIII and Elizabeth restricted the felling of trees by law to save the timber for the Navy. It took two thousand prime oaks to construct one large ship. Vast trunks were hauled out of the Weald to the Chatham yards. Defoe in 1720 wrote, 'the timber I saw was prodigious, as well in quantity as in bigness, and sometimes I have seen one tree on a carriage drawn by twenty-two oxen, and even then it is carried so little a way, and then thrown down, and left for other tugs to take up and carry on, that sometimes it is two or three years before it gets to Chatham, for sometimes a whole summer is not dry enough to make the roads passable.'

Still, the oaks survive supreme everywhere, often of stupendous size and age, like that in Headcorn's churchyard or in the garden of Sissinghurst Place, but more often they are found as standards in a coppice of hazel or sweet chestnut which is cut for palings in a rotation of every twelve years or so, allowing the wild flowers to spring up astonishingly after their long slumber. The beech is the second-ranked Wealden tree, of which the best examples are at Toys Hill, near Sevenoaks, where the beeches form so dense a canopy that nothing grows beneath them and walking was an unimpeded delight until the devastating storm of October 1987.

We who live in the Weald have been very fortunate. Our countryside was shaped by historical chance, and preserved by it. We were spared industrialization except at the only period when its buildings were visual assets. We have been bypassed by major

*The apple harvest at Four Wents, near Hawkhurst, in the heart of the Weald.*

routes, and the roads follow twisting and often deeply cloven courses down hillsides where branches touch overhead to form leafy tunnels. We are much visited, but have no resorts except Tunbridge Wells. We have kept our woodlands, and on the whole our fields.

There is no conflict between town and country. The Weald has not become a backwater. It is thriving, experimental. Modern development and changes in building materials are often assets. For example, the Bewl Bridge Reservoir is delightfully harmonious in a countryside which lacked a large lake, and the occasional industrial buildings, like those recently erected outside Staplehurst station, or High Halden's new housing, arouse no justifiable protest. To preserve the Weald's serenity, it is not necessary to imitate the past. The past did not imitate its past. How strange the Elizabethan tower at Sissinghurst Castle must have looked when first erected, or the folly at Hadlow, or a Georgian house like Hendon Hall in Biddenden or Westwell in Tenterden, or the cowled oast houses when they were added to nineteenth-century farms! None of these buildings were indigenous to the Weald, but they fitted it aesthetically. Yet our ancestors lacked the checks and advantages now available to us – a national concern for the environment, Acts of Parliament to control our excesses, planning regulations, new

*The brick tower, or folly, at Hadlow was built in 1840 outside Hadlow Court Castle by Walter May. It is octagonal, telescoping upwards in four storeys to a height of one hundred and seventy feet – an astonishing feature to rise above the Weald.*

building techniques, architects, good road surfaces, lorries, rail, and watchdogs like the Weald of Kent Preservation Society. The builders of the churches and houses bequeathed to us from the twelfth to the eighteenth centuries were almost illiterate. Bad communications confined them to a tiny corner of Britain so that they never saw what was being built elsewhere, and the reputation of Wealden roads kept strangers out. But they had something which one can only define as instinctive taste.

Have we lost it? Undoubtedly we are guilty of blemishes in what we do to our properties or allow others to do to theirs. You can see examples in almost every village, at the turn of almost every lane – television aerials whiskering cottage roofs when they could be put inside, metallic litter around farmyards, or additions made in

*Above: Coppices are a perennial feature of Kent. Once every twelve years the trees are cut for palings, leaving oaks as standards to provide sturdier timber.*

*Left: After the oak the Weald's most common tree is the beech. This tree stands near Seal, and behind it are chestnuts in their first year of regrowth after coppicing.*

unsympathetic materials, a door painted bright pink, a shabby shop-front brutally extruded to break the line of a village street, oversize signs on garages and chain stores dictated by some remote headquarters (there is a terrible example in Lydd), wires led down a street instead of behind it, double yellow lines on narrow roads, crudely designed notices outside and inside churches and village halls, rows of plastic sheeting on horticultural crops, motorcycle rallies in quiet fields, a derelict caravan abandoned for years outside a cottage. One could prolong the list indefinitely. Visual good manners are as important to a community as social good manners, and we must steel ourselves to be indignant guardians of the beauty we have inherited.

I must not end on this critical note. I think of a narrow lane near Hawkhurst which dips sharply to a stream. In the valley bottom lie two houses, one each side of the lane and linked by the stream, which was dammed on the upper side to form a small lake and on the other turned the great wooden wheel of a flour mill. The latter house is still called Slip Mill, the other Primrose Hill. Both are trimly white, both have lovely gardens, and both are samples of what the Weald offers so plentifully to people who care for it, the one a perfect adaptation of a functional building, the other a symbol of the serene privacy that was won from the old forest, its flowering terraces descending to the water.

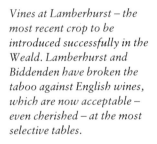

*Vines at Lamberhurst – the most recent crop to be introduced successfully in the Weald. Lamberhurst and Biddenden have broken the taboo against English wines, which are now acceptable – even cherished – at the most selective tables.*

# 3

# *The Marshes*

KENT HAS NO offshore islands, if you define an island as a chunk of land approachable only by water. But it does have four coastal segments, Romney Marsh, Thanet, Sheppey and the Hundred of Hoo, which to this day retain something akin to insularity. Thanet and Sheppey were actual islands until the channels narrowed and could be bridged. Romney Marsh is an enclosed bay of the sea, and the Hoo a peninsula between the Thames and the Medway.

Romney Marsh, one of the strangest districts of Britain, is easily accessible and yet remote, and has attached to it (one can scarcely say part of it) Dungeness, a triangular shoulder created in recent centuries by the scouring of shingle, a promontory large and distinctive enough to show up on a world map. The Marsh is composed of large polygonal fields separated by straight dykes. There is no feeling of being in Kent. To someone flying south from Maidstone, the contrast with the High Weald is immediate. The wooded hills, tight little fields and villages suddenly give way to a flat jigsaw land of contiguous lozenges, spotted with barns and isolated houses. At ground level one observes intensive cultivation, and wonders how so large an expanse of farmland, with its complicated crops and drainage, can be managed by so sparse a population.

To its devotees the Marsh has a magical quality, a great expanse of sky, 'a feeling of boundless space, a solemn stillness', as Richard Ingrams has described it, but it is a taste that can only slowly be acquired by those who prefer the fluffier, bouncier country of the Weald. The Marsh can be bleak. Mist often lies low over it, and in winter cruel winds sweep across unimpeded. Its best moment is in the spring, when fields of yellow rape alternate with great pastures grazed by sheep and lambs. Then the marsh gains variety, a domestic sweetness, almost an intimacy. Its very existence impels first curiosity, then admiration, exceptionally love. No such terrain could be natural. It was won from the sea. But how?

Romney Marsh proper is only the northern half of the total area of fifty thousand acres, but has given its name in popular speech to

*Previous page: Although much of Romney Marsh is still grazing land, it is increasingly ploughed for corn, rape, vegetables (in this case, leeks and sprouts), and even tulips. For so intensively cultivated an area, it is very sparsely populated.*

*Right above: Romney Marsh at sheep's eye level. The dyke, or 'sewer', is part of the elaborate drainage system, begun before the Norman Conquest, which transformed the sea-bed into the most fertile land in England.*

*Right below: Old Romney typifies the contrast between the size and antiquity of the churches on Romney Marsh and the relative scarcity of the secular buildings they served. Although the present church at Old Romney is Norman and haphazard additions were added in later centuries, its once-island site is Saxon.*

the whole. The other sections are Walland Marsh, Denge Marsh and the Guildeford Level, stretching towards Rye. In remote ages, when temporarily the land rose above the sea, it was forested, and balks of sodden timber are still found twenty feet deep in the alluvium which created it. Then the forest was drowned, and long before man intervened to control the waters, there was a slow cycle of submergence and consolidation as the sea beaches built up and river silt was deposited. It produced at the time of the Roman invasion a wide bay spotted with islands like Lydd, Oxney and Old Romney, and crossed by the meandering River Rother which then emptied into the sea at Romney. Dungeness did not exist, even embryonically. The Roman fort at Lympne was sited on an inlet of the sea, and many other creeks, some salt water, some fresh, gave them access as far inland as Appledore and Smallhythe. The rest of the bay was mud flat at low water, covered by the high tides, a hideous waterscape which the Romans never attempted to drain. Until recently it was conjectured that they constructed the first sea wall each side of Dymchurch, and reclaimed Romney Marsh by means of the Rhee Wall which extends from Appledore to Romney, but modern research has disproved it. There is nothing Roman about the Marsh except the ruins of their Portus Lemanis (Lympne), a small settlement at Dymchurch, and a single Mithraic altar found at Stone in Oxney.

The firm shoreline of the bay was the edge of the Weald. It rises on the northern edge of the Marsh, running through Aldington, Warehorn and Appledore, and forming a gentle cliff from which the whole extent of the Marsh can be viewed. The first artificial dykes and walls were made before and after the Norman Conquest, by which time the natural shift of shingle on the beaches and the consolidation of the land by river silt had made it possible to hold it firm by the construction of the Rhee Wall, a waterway between two banks. It is first mentioned in documents of 1258. In addition to draining the Marsh, it served as a canal between Appledore and the sea, and scoured clear the harbour of New Romney. The Domesday Book and other records mention eleven churches on the reclaimed land.

The alluvium was found to be so fertile, and is still today the richest soil in Britain, that the Archbishops of Canterbury, who owned most of it, found it worthwhile to reclaim Walland Marsh as well. To some extent, this ground had already dried out naturally, but they had to exclude the tides by strengthening the natural beaches, then construct dykes or 'sewers' to drain it. This colossal task, carried out mainly by monks, resulted in the reclamation of the entire area by the early Middle Ages. Their difficulty was all the greater because the Marsh lies below the level of high tides, and

*The interior of Old Romney Church is delightfully cool and simple. This is the north chapel: the lancet window is thirteenth-century, and the twisted balusters of the altar rail are Queen Anne.*

slopes gently inland from the sea instead of towards it. The lowest land lies at the foot of Appledore, which remained marshy and unhealthy until the Royal Military Canal was dug in 1809. The sea sluices had to be closed at every high tide and the surface water pumped mechanically to a level where it could escape. It was an amazing feat of engineering at a time when the machinery and the knowledge of hydraulics were primitive.

Their achievement was almost destroyed as soon as completed. The reclamation of the Marsh had the unexpected effect of blocking the harbours by the accumulation of silt which could not now escape fast enough, and the exclusion of the sea forced the shingle eastwards to build the promontory of Dungeness. That was not the worst. Violent storms in the thirteenth century destroyed the ports. Winchelsea was totally submerged, and New Romney suffered almost as great a catastrophe when the tempest of 1287 levelled the houses and choked the harbour mouth. The water stains can still be seen several feet up the interior pillars of the church. The violence of the storm also altered the course of the Rother, which found its new, and present, outlet close to Rye. So New Romney, the chief of

the Cinque Ports, lost its harbour, and now lies a mile from the sea.

By Tudor times the Marsh had gained its present shape and to a large degree its present appearance. In 1586 William Camden wrote: 'None but those who have seen it can believe how rich the soil is, what great herds of cattle it feeds, which are driven here to fatten from the furthest part of England, or with what art it is embanked against the sea.' But it was not a pleasant place to live in. Lambarde described it as 'evil in winter, grievous in summer, and never good', and the contrast between is fecundity and its dreariness has remained characteristic. Away from the coast there is only one true village, Brookland. The other settlements are hamlets, and the scattered farms seldom include a building earlier than the eighteenth century. There are no houses of a size or dignity to warrant the name of manor or mansion. It is a district which suggests absentee landlords.

The exceptions are the churches. It is extraordinary how many of them were built in a largely empty land. Thirteen survive, and there were once half-a-dozen more. What can have been the purpose? As the Marsh was largely owned by Canterbury until the Reformation,

*Woods used frequently to act as boundaries, and this bank near Smallhythe probably represents the edge of one such vanished medieval wood.*

*Romney Marsh has thirteen surviving medieval churches, and another half-dozen are known to have existed. Fairfield church, probably Norman in origin and later cased in brick, now stands a long way from any village, and the famous sheep graze right up to the walls.*

there would have been a natural tendency for the Archbishops to stamp their authority on the land, to celebrate significantly each new triumph of reclamation, perhaps to provide a vertical feature in so much flatness as a guide for travellers, and to allow for a hoped-for increase in population. The difficulty of building these churches was immense. There was no stone nearer than Hythe, no timber except from the Weald, and to transport these materials there were only boggy tracks crossing at intervals of a few hundred yards dykes which were constantly liable to flood. The only labour available were monks and peasants forced to abandon their ceaseless work on the crops, pastures and drainage. The ground was unstable for building, and their techniques primitive.

It is therefore with wonder that one discovers a church like Old Romney's, standing on a slight rise between fields of grazing sheep, with only a few cottages at a distance, to find within it a Norman nave and a perfect crown-post roof, a gallery on Doric columns, a ladder stair of unimaginable antiquity and a great chunk of thirteenth-century stone as a font. The church could seat three hundred, but the total local population could never have numbered more than fifty. Even more remarkable for its isolation is Fairfield church, which has no hamlet at all and stands on the level marsh which still sometimes floods around it. Timber-framed and roofed, it was later cased in red and blue brick, and inside there are white box pews and a three-decker pulpit, giving this exquisite miniature building an elegance which is totally unexpected.

Then there is Brookland church, larger, grander, with an extraordinary detached belfry built round huge vertical beams and roofed by three overlapping octagonal caps; St Mary in the Marsh, its tower Norman, its Early English interior delightfully cool and bare; Ivychurch, a nave completely devoid of pews; Brenzett, also Norman, one of the few to be sheathed by trees; and Newchurch, which has a leaning tower which has somehow managed to settle short of collapse. All these churches are medieval, some originally Saxon, and hardly touched by the Renaissance or the Victorians. A local society has undertaken the formidable task, in default of adequate congregations, of keeping them in repair, and their efforts have preserved the Marsh's greatest legacy – apart from one other, its agriculture.

It is above all famous for the special breed of sheep which was probably first imported by the Flemings. They are white-faced, Roman-nosed, sturdy, as they need to be to tolerate the icy winds and sogginess underfoot. Romney Marsh sheep graze in thousands over twenty-acre fields, not congregating in family groups, as sheep are supposed to do, but set apart, individually and everlastingly munching. The grass is so rich that the best of it can fatten six or ten sheep per acre, compared to two on the Downs, and the rams are exported all over the world. The sheep are the Marsh's staple crop, its heraldic beast. But they have been joined by cattle, and the pastures are increasingly ploughed up for corn, rape, vegetables, fruit and even tulips. This is the farmer's perennial dilemma. Why devote such richness to raising livestock when it could be used even more profitably for crops? When Cobbett passed this way in 1823, he liked the sheep ('very pretty and large'), but it was the corn that aroused his greater admiration. 'I never saw corn like this before. They reap the wheat here nearly two foot from the ground; and even then they cut it three feet long!' In his day there was much more pasture than arable. The big change came with the two world wars. Cereal was needed more than meat and wool, and the area under plough increased fourfold. Today nearly half the Marsh is tilled, not to its disadvantage visually, for the changing colours of the crops alternate on a grand scale with the white-dotted pastures. In May the whole expanse is alive with growth and movement, and the air is filled with the croaking of rooks and innumerable frogs.

I have explained that Romney Marsh has had in effect four coasts

*Port Lympne (pronounced 'Lim') overlooks Romney Marsh from the steep escarpment which in Roman days formed the cliff-shore of a vast bay. Sir Philip Sassoon transformed an old manor house on this site in 1912, creating a millionaire's mansion where he lavishly entertained the leading politicians of the inter-war years.*

– the prehistoric cliff face which marks its northern boundary, the old shoreline which retreated a mile seaward to close the harbours, the present beaches, and Dungeness. Of these, the first is the most attractive. Villages like Warehorn and Appledore, a few great houses like Lympne Castle and Port Lympne, lie on the very edge of it. Appledore is perhaps the prettiest of the villages. Its ancient church and separated houses enclose a wide street which passes between two of them to lead down to the Marsh, and the rosiness of the brick and tile complements the white weather-boarding in a manner which is distinctively Kentish. Nearby rises the Isle of Oxney, a piece of the Weald floated clear, overlooking the Marsh but in no sense part of it, with wiggly lanes thickly treed and vegetated. At Wittersham, in other respects too straggly a village and too recently expanded to charm, there is an old church caressed by a great lime, and a Lutyenized mansion opposite it. But the best of Oxney is Stone, where the church has as its neighbour a lovely timbered house, and from its glebe field the view, the whole way to Dungeness, is the most spectactular on the whole perimeter of the Marsh.

*Above: Hythe lies on the eastern edge of Romney Marsh. Because of the coastal plain which slowly built up during the Middle Ages to deprive it of its port, the prettily cottaged lanes reach up the slope of the cliff from the busy transverse streets below.*

*Left: An outpost of the Weald, Appledore lies on the rim of the cliff descending steeply to Romney Marsh. The Vikings landed here in 892 in strength, to be repulsed by Alfred the Great.*

On the 'intermediate' coastline, Lydd, New Romney and Hythe were left stranded by the retreat of the sea. Lydd is wonderful, my favourite small Kentish town after Sandwich. Its few streets of excellent small houses and shops, differently coloured by their materials or at the whim of the owner, lead here and there into open spaces, the largest of which is occupied by one of the loveliest (and incidentally the longest) churches in England, originally Saxon, its pale stone gently crumbling. Not the least memorable event in its long history is that its chancel was totally destroyed by a German bomb in 1940, and has been restored with a sympathy that is beyond praise. New Romney is less pleasing, its High Street commercialized, its shop fascias discordant, but its church, once the spiritual headquarters of the Cinque Ports, is a marvellous Norman building with a chunky tower and heavy internal columns, alternately round and octagonal, that lead one into the graceful

fourteenth-century chancel, a perfect fusion of two architectural styles. North from here, the towns approach the beach – Littlestone, St Mary's Bay and Dymchurch, ribbon-developed along fine sands and guarded by a great sea-wall. At Hythe, nicely terraced where the ground begins to rise again, there are bustling streets and another fine church. This coast, let it be admitted, is not beautiful, too flat and adulterated by buildings unworthy of their predecessors, and its gauntness is accentuated by its most remarkable feature – Dungeness.

The story of this most recent addition to the English coastline has been admirably told in Walter J.C. Murray's *Romney Marsh*, and is too complicated to repeat here. In brief, this huge triangular beach was formed, and is still being enlarged, by the movement of shingle eastwards from the Sussex headlands, where it originates as flints torn by sea action from the chalk cliffs. No part of it existed until Romney Marsh was reclaimed, and then the beach gradually built up in successive bands of shingle between Lydd and New Romney. The thirteenth-century storms hastened the process. The shingle was deposited, layer on layer (one can still trace the slight undulations) on the south beach, very little of it on the east, at a rate which could add eight or ten feet of beach a year. The scouring is so intense that the water deepens to sixty feet within a hundred yards, and large ships can navigate astonishingly close inshore.

Evidence of the rapid accumulation of the shingle is seen in the position of the four successive lighthouses. The first was built in 1615, the second in 1792, the third (which you can still climb to the top) in 1904, each abandoned in turn as the shoreline advanced beyond it. The latest, most elegant and technically perfect, was finished in 1960. The lighthouse keepers were joined in their vigil by fishermen who drew up their boats on the beach, as they still do, and then by outsiders who found in this desolation an attractiveness unappealing to most of us, and built for themselves beach huts, which became more elaborate, but no less shoddy, as they decided to occupy them permanently. Between the wars, more and more trippers found Dungeness an unusual destination for a day's outing, and when the miniature railway was extended from Hythe and Dymchurch in 1929 to make the Ness its terminus, they came in their thousands, thus destroying the loneliness which they had come to see.

*The successive beaches or 'fulls' at Dungeness were created by storm action over many centuries, and they form the most remarkable shingle promontory in the world. The shingle continues to accumulate year by year, and buildings which were at one time coastal – including lighthouses – have gradually been left hundreds of yards inland.*

The final and most incongruous additions to the scene were the two vast nuclear power stations that dominate the blunt point of the headland, and are visible from every part of Romney Marsh and the surrounding hills. They were sited here because twenty million gallons of cooling water per hour could easily be drawn from the deep channel and discharged, slightly hotter, back into the sea. Some people find them magnificent technological castles, a thin pennant of steam substituting for a flag. To others they are visual outrages on what they paradoxically call 'a very human landscape', spoiling their enjoyment of the birds. The birds do not seem to mind. I take an intermediate position. Dungeness was never human or beautiful, and the power stations have a certain appropriateness in a place where nature itself has turned bizarre. From a distance they can look beautiful in the lifting mist. I only regret the pairs of

*The giant nuclear power stations on Dungeness, built in 1965 and 1968 on the very edge of the promontory, are thought by some conservationists to be a brutal invasion of a desolate spot, by others to be a brilliant manifestation of twentieth-century technology on an ideal site.*

pylons that stride from them across the Marsh, breaking its flat melancholy.

Thanet, unlike Romney Marsh, has a cliff-girt coast, now crusted with the resort towns that stretch round the nub of the North Foreland. It was once a genuine island, separated from the Kentish mainland by the Wantsum, which from Roman till Tudor times was a short-cut shipping lane from the Channel to the Thames estuary. Two rivers, the Great and Little Stour, entered it at a place still called Stourmouth, and at either end, at Richborough and Reculver, the Romans built their forts. For thirteen centuries the Wantsum remained navigable by large ships, but was gradually narrowed by the accumulation of sand and shingle washed down from the northern mouth, until in the late fifteenth century it was finally closed. The united Stours flowed across the ancient channel bed, twisted into a great loop north of Sandwich to enter the sea at Pegwell Bay. Technically, Thanet is still an island. You could canoe from Reculver along a wandering dyke called euphemistically the River Wantsum, until it joins the Stour near Sarre, but the waterway is so slight that you would certainly miss it driving fast from Herne Bay to Margate. Only the Ordnance Survey map reveals Thanet's continuing insularity.

When the channel was clear from sea to sea, the island was of great commercial importance, and its history, for so small a patch of land, formidable. From the higher ground near Manston airfield you can see on a fine day the site of Richborough, the twin towers of Reculver, Ebbsfleet where St Augustine, and Hengist and Horsa, landed, Kingsgate which the Vikings invaded and, in the far distance, Canterbury, which pulled all these historical strings together. Throughout the Dark and Middle Ages the coastal towns, which occupied themselves with fishing and smuggling, were of less importance than Sarre, Monkton and Minster, all lying on the Thanet side of the Wantsum, and especially Minster, which became a busy port for trans-Channel traffic. There was no bridge over the Wantsum till 1485, but the ferry at Sarre did duty for one, and at St Nicholas at Wade, as the name indicates, the creek was actually fordable at low tide.

As the channel slowly closed, the resulting marshland was reclaimed for agriculture and enriched by seaweed, and with Romney Marsh it was known as the most productive land in England. Caxton, who was born in the Weald and whose regional accent is implicit in his unorthodox spelling, called it, 'Thanatos, that is Tenet, a ylonde besydes Kent and hath the name Thanatos, of deth of serpentes, for ther ben none. Ther is a noble corn lond and fruytful.' The legend about the absence of snakes cannot be upheld, but when the villages ceased to be inland ports, they gained immeasurably from the fertility of the reclaimed land. Until the Reformation most of it was owned by the Church, then by lay landlords who farmed it in large estates. The remaining woodland was cleared, and it was spotted with windmills. It was found to be ideal pastureland for Romney Marsh sheep, and by 1700 three times more land was grazed then ploughed. Then, as on Romney Marsh, arable once more gained the ascendancy, and when Cobbett came here in 1823, he found it 'a country of corn. . . . All was corn around me. Barns, I should think two hundred feet long, ricks of enormous size and most numerous, crops of wheat five quarters to an acre on the average.' But the labourers were beggarly poor. 'In this beautiful island,' Cobbett goes on, 'every inch of land is appropriated by the rich. No hedges, no ditches, no commons, no grassy lanes . . . and the wretched labourer has not a stick of wood and no place for a pig or cow to graze.'

No ditches! The low land is threaded by them. Since Cobbett's day the land use has again changed. Much of coastal Thanet has been swallowed by the encroaching towns, and vegetable crops have largely succeeded corn and sheep inland. The villages no longer suffer from the selfishness of a few. Employment is diversified. The resorts draw in seasonal workers. Chislet was the northernmost Kent colliery until closed in 1970. The farms are mechanized. Everything, and everyone, appears smiling. St Nicholas at Wade is neat and tree-girt round a large church, Sarre a pleasant village of old brick houses, famous for its Crown Inn. Minster is the grandest, with a superb church of flint and stone, and a little distance away is Minster Abbey, founded in 670, sacked by Vikings, rebuilt by Normans, and now occupied by nuns who fled Bavaria in 1937 to settle in this idyllic spot and farm the surrounding land.

The Isle of Sheppey is divided from the mainland by the Swale, a broad tidal channel which gives us a good idea of the appearance of the Wantsum before it was lost in the Thanet marshes. There are no longer any ferry-crossings to Sheppey, and land access is by a single bridge north of Sittingbourne, an extraordinary structure, like an inverted table, of four tall pylons that between them lift the road and railway for the passage of ships. Once on the island, you cross low-lying land, scruffy with dereliction and wind-blown grass, which rises pleasingly to a ridge of clay hills to the north.

There are only three towns of importance on Sheppey – Queenborough, Sheerness and Minster. Queenborough, called after Edward III's Queen Philippa, once had a castle, now reduced to a few grassy bumps, and by 1670, when Defoe visited the place, it

*Like Romney Marsh and the low-lying parts of Thanet, the marshland on the Isle of Sheppey was won from the sea to create agricultural land. The rough pastures, intersected by dykes, form the loneliest and most mournful acreages in the south-east of England, hence they are a favourite resort for rare sea birds.*

was 'a miserable, dirty, decayed, poor, pitiful fishing town' (but he said much the same of delectable Sandwich), and it revived only in the eighteenth century when a single street, of fine brick houses and a Guildhall, was built above the quays. This is still the most pleasant part of Queenborough, a neat example of Georgian gentility sentimentalized by associations with Nelson and Emma Hamilton, but parallel to it is a ditch of a creek, ghastly at low tide with steep mud banks, shabby boats and industrial waste, the marine equivalent of a neglected farmyard. A jetty snakes forlornly across the mud into the Swale.

Sheerness is more remarkable, not for its town, which is almost wholly Victorian, but for its dockyard. It was first laid out by Pepys in 1665, but nothing of his plan remains, as it was totally and excellently rebuilt in the early nineteenth century, with warehouses, a garrison church, the Captain's House, and various stores and workshops, all in pale brick with stone dressings expertly jointed and fenestrated in Regency proportions. The best of the functional buildings (1859) is the Boat Store, one of the earliest in the country to have a cast-iron framework, four storeys high with bands of small identical windows, and inside as grand as a cathedral nave, a

*Men dig for lug-worms (a favourite angler's bait) at Leysdown on the Isle of Sheppey. At low tide the bait-diggers wander far from the shore, bending over their shallow trenches.*

huge space with tiered galleries like clerestories on each side. All these buildings were continually in use by the Fleet until 1959. Now the dockyard has been surrendered to commercial shipping. Vast metal warehouses have recently been added, whole docks filled in to provide standing room for the Toyotas off-loaded from chunky Japanese ships, and one quay is allotted to the daily vehicle ferry to Flushing. It is a vibrant harbour, Kent's second busiest after Dover, but as carefully guarded from tourist intrusion, because of bonded warehousing, as it was in its days of naval secrecy.

Minster was Sheppey's original settlement, its Abbey founded in 664, and after its destruction by the Danes rebuilt in the twelfth century as a Benedictine nunnery. The stone gatehouse is lovely, and the church stands splendidly on top of a hill, still bearing traces of its Saxon origins, with Roman tiles embedded in the walls. But Sheppey's towns are disappointing, sprawling and spattered with advertisement. Towards its north-east end, holiday resorts like Warden and Leysdown provide more entertainment than visual delight. The island's fame is due to the great marshes which extend along its southern half from end to end, marshes in fact no longer, for like Romney, Thanet and the Hoo, they were drained centuries ago, the water gathered into convenient field-dividing channels. Sheppey means 'island of sheep', but you see few sheep there today. Once again, the land has been found more valuable as arable, and the corn spreads in August over vast acreages like a lion's pelt. In winter it is bleak, and the widely separated farms provide the only note of domesticity. There is a modern prison south of Eastchurch, one of its least offensive buildings, and in the far south-east corner, Harty church, the most remote in Kent, unattached to any village, and an inn, the terminal of the ferry that once plied across the Swale to Faversham. This, and neighbouring Elmley Island, a nature reserve, is the part of Sheppey which few people explore, but the most rewarding for its fruitfulness, its birds, its isolation and its strangeness. It is said that there are still people born here who have never crossed the Swale to the mainland.

The most notable buildings in the Hoo peninsula are the church at Cliffe and nearby Cooling Castle, and its most spectacular view is obtained between them across the Thames estuary. This is Dickens country. He lived for the last fifteen years of his life at Gadshill, near Higham, and set the famous opening scene of *Great Expectations*, when Pip encounters the escaped convict, in the churchyard of Cooling church: 'The flat dark wilderness beyond the churchyard, intersected with dykes and mounds and gates, with scattered cattle feeding on it, was the marshes; and the low, leaden line beyond was the river; and the distant savage lair from which the wind was rushing was the sea.' It is a little different now. The church is still there, with the five miniature grave stones which Dickens describes (actually ten, but he didn't want to strain credulity), all children of the Comport family who died in the 1770s of a marsh plague, none of them surviving beyond seventeen months. The marsh is also there, now richly grazed and cultivated, and so is the river, but on the Essex shore circular oil cisterns now stand in mile-long rows, catching the setting sun like crescent moons.

Cooling Castle, once the home of Sir John Oldcastle on whom Shakespeare modelled Falstaff, is a stupendous edifice to find in so desolate a place. Its gateway, flanked by two rotund towers and deeply machicolated, is in a more unadulterated condition than almost any other secular monument of the fourteenth century. The double moat and the curtain walls of the outer and inner baileys also survive in places, the walls sometimes to a great height, but the living quarters do not. They have been replaced by a modernized house, some think incongruously, because a suburban villa looks odd within so magnificent a portal, and a splendid barn stands in the outer bailey. Children play on interior lawns. It is very peaceful. High up on one of the gateway towers is a copper tablet, placed

there in 1381 by its owner, John de Cobham, which proclaims that he built it 'in help of the cuntre' as a defence against the French. But Cooling was never put to this test. Instead, it was attacked by Sir Thomas Wyatt in 1554 in the course of his ill-fated revolt against Queen Mary, and the then Lord Cobham, Wyatt's uncle, surrendered the castle ignominiously after a siege of only six hours, pleading shortage of cannon and the lukewarm support of his henchmen. He only just escaped execution on Tower Hill. Wyatt didn't.

Cliffe church is even older, thirteenth-century, remodelled in the fourteenth. Its walls are alternate bands of ragstone and flint, and its porch, large enough to hold the entire population, is of the same pleasing combination. The whole lavish edifice is an amazing monument in so poor a village.

The Hoo (the name means 'promontory', between the two great rivers which shape it) has one other building of note, immense and spectacular. A creek formerly isolated the eastern end of the peninsula which is still known as the Isle of Grain, not for its produce but for its gravelly shore. It was an abandoned sort of place, known only for a tiny railway station and quay where Queen Victoria often embarked on the *Victoria and Albert* to escape the crowds at more frequented ports. It had but one village, Grain. Then, in 1959, the island was taken over by B.P. for the refining and storage of oil, brought to its jetties by huge tankers. The storage drums are impressive in their massed battalions, but the latest addition to this extraordinary terminus is a vast building which compares favourably with the greatest achievements of modern British architecture, the Grain power station. Five massive generators, fuelled by oil and sheathed in metal that gleams like aluminium, stand at equal intervals along the shore, and beside them rises an immensely tall chimney that flares bulbously at its base like a lighthouse. This is the answer to Dungeness, proclaiming across the whole width of the combined estuaries not just a triumph of technology but of design.

The Hoo has been described as 'an out-of-the-way, wild sort of place, in which, unless obliged to do so, people did not live'. That does it an injustice. Much of it is flat and featureless, dull beet fields under a uniformly grey sky. But it has its hills, its wooded knolls, its heronry near High Halstow, and for its historical and literary associations, its ancient and modern monuments, it deserves not just a day's visit, but an exploration.

*The oil-fuelled power station on the Isle of Grain is the finest work of modern architecture in Kent. Designed by Farmer & Dark in the 1970s, it is the largest of its kind in Europe. The five generators produce enough electricity to meet the needs of three cities the size of Birmingham.*

95

# 4

# *Country Houses*

IT IS NATURAL that Kent should possess a greater number and a greater variety of country houses than any other county, lying as it does between London and the Channel ports, within easy reach of both, and having enjoyed throughout the centuries an affluence based on agriculture which created an exceptionally beautiful countryside. In this chapter I shall be dealing with the major houses, but it is well to remember that Kent has also inherited a very large number of smaller manor houses, particularly of the Wealden type. Their timber frames, bricks and tiles of differently pleasing reds, and their universal gardens, are among the chief delights the county can offer, particularly when you come upon them unexpectedly, pulling up the car with a squeal of brakes and pleasure. It is because they are so much loved by wealthy owners that they have been so well preserved and modernized, continuing the tradition that Londoners seek in Kent a refuge from the metropolis.

However, Kent lacks vast estates, and of houses on a Chatsworth scale there are only three – Knole, Otford and Cobham – all pre-seventeenth century, and one now ruined. There were dukes but no dukeries. At the Dissolution, the great possessions of Canterbury's two foundations, Christ Church and St Augustine's, were divided into relatively small pieces between yeomen and existing landlords. Such estates as were created were in scattered manors concentrated in a single ownership, like the forty-two in Kent and Sussex acquired by Sir John Baker of Sissinghurst. As time passed, ancestral money was forfeited or wasted, or the direct line of inheritance failed, and these individual properties were sold to their tenants or outsiders, leaving a patchwork of freehold farms and manors which characterizes the rural part of the county to this day.

*Previous page: Sissinghurst Castle was once a major Tudor and Elizabethan house, built around two courtyards. Two-thirds of it was pulled down in about 1800, leaving only the brick tower and isolated fragments to form the framework of the famous garden created here from 1930 onwards.*

But here and there a few farms might be amalgamated to form a park, and a great house set in it. The favoured districts were the agriculturally richest and most beautiful, especially round Maidstone, Sevenoaks and in the Weald, but even in a windswept and scenically unrewarding place like Sheppey one finds Shurland (alas in ruins) or Gadshill in the Hundred of Hoo. The coast was avoided until Lord Holland built his extraordinary Holland House in the 1760s, a stone's throw from the North Foreland, for views were considered less of an amenity than snugness in a fold of pastoral land enclosed by great woods, a serpentine drive approaching the house between them. Kent was never very adventurous architecturally. It followed fashion, but at an interval. Its houses are very English, with little trace of foreign influence apart from the classical (Mereworth is the supreme example), despite the nearness of mainland Europe. The character of the people, and of its buildings, is traditional.

The county lacked a good building stone, the great quarries round Maidstone yielding only Kentish rag, which is porous, crumbles quickly, easily picks up dirt and is difficult to cut into regular shapes. In compensation Kent had excellent brick from its claylands, and at first a limitless supply of timber. The lack of good roads, until they were turnpiked in the late eighteenth century, made transport of materials difficult. The appalling state of the Wealden roads in winter became a joke among travellers, and the only maintenance they received was an annual ploughing. There were rivers which could carry stone and timber – the Medway as far as Tonbridge and the Stour to Canterbury – but only one canal, between Gravesend and Rochester, which failed.

The building of so many medium-sized houses and churches deep in the county therefore represents a considerable feat of organization and portage. Look at a map of Kent in the eighteenth century, like Andrews', on the scale of two inches to the mile, which shows every barn, every spinney, every lane existing at that date, and you will observe how completely the land was populated, and how the larger houses, all labelled on the map with their owners' names, lie companionably alongside their neighbours, doctor with Earl, a knight's widow with a lawyer, scarcely a field separating them. It was an aristocratic society. Many of the houses remained for centuries in the hands of the same family. And when you examine, in Harris's or Hasted's county histories, the illustrations of these houses, drawn not as sketches but with an architect's care for detail, you see how neat even the smallest of them were, how tonsured their gardens and surrounding orchards, and the only evidence of the inconveniences of life is sometimes a rutted road by which a coach crawls laboriously towards the house. It is certainly an

*The range of medieval buildings at Penshurst Place seen from the garden. The large window on the left lies at the end of the long gallery; next to it is the Buckingham Building; then come the solar, the Baron's Hall, and, on the right, one of the garden towers.*

idealized picture. The subscribers to these lavish volumes were the owners of the houses, which they wished to see illustrated in their most flattering guise. There is no suggestion of how miserably the poor were living at their gates, that crops often failed, streams overflowed their banks and barns fell derelict. It is seldom that a house is shown altered, a wing added or amputated, but we know that this was constantly done.

Comparing Andrews' map with the modern Ordnance Survey, one discovers how many of these houses are lost to us, decayed, demolished, burnt or swallowed by industrial or suburban sprawl. When so much survives, it seems almost niggardly to regret their loss. But looking at Jan Siberecht's idyllic painting of Bifrons near Patrixbourne, pulled down as recently as 1948, or remembering Lynstead and Bayhall, of which only fragments survive, or Eastwell Park, or Ford Place where only a wing still stands, one knows that architectural masterpieces have perished that can never be replaced, for the art form itself has been abandoned. It is not likely that large country houses will ever be built again.

In this summary, let us start with Penshurst Place, because it is one of Kent's oldest and greatest houses and represents a continuity of family (the Sidneys) and a constant adaptation to meet old needs with new methods. It was built in 1341 by a London merchant as a vast hall house, an expansion of the yeoman's typical house on a baronial scale, with a hall sixty-two feet long roofed by chestnut beams, and at one end of it, approached by a stone stairway that a man could mount on horseback, is a long solar with an undercroft below. Later, a majestic apartment, the Buckingham Building, was added, and turrets to the circuit of the property. In Tudor and Elizabethan times, the Sidneys built brick wings to connect with some of them, incorporating the loveliest long gallery in England and the chamber where Philip Sidney was born. But it is to the great hall, a barn glorified, a nave secularized, that one always returns, the largest unaltered medieval hall except Westminster's, more splendid than the halls at Wye College and Lympne Castle, and authentic to its original tiled floor, its gallery above the screen, its central hearth, and the long oak table where the retainers sat below the master's dais.

Knole comes next in order of priority, in date, not size, for it is much larger than Penshurst, a fifteenth-century palace built by Thomas Bouchier, Archbishop of Canterbury, round the tiny nucleus of an earlier manor house. It lies outside Sevenoaks in a thousand-acre park planted with beech and sweet chestnut and grazed by dainty deer. It is a grey, sober house of Kentish ragstone, and rises from the green of the park like some medieval town. Large enough for an archbishop, it was not large enough for Henry VIII, who sequestered it from Canterbury and added the Green Court in front of Bouchier's house, surrounding it by apartments broken by the central entrance tower. Knole must then have looked rather forbidding. It was still essentially Gothic. Then it was given by Queen Elizabeth to her cousin and first minister, Thomas Sackville, and in a few years he transformed it. To the range facing the park, to the garden front and inside the Green Court, he added curly gables surmounted by his family crest, the leopard, an act of grace that changed the bleak exteriors into façades of appealing charm. His alterations inside part of the house were less successful. They coincided with a short-lived phase of English design imitative of the Flemish, too crudely carved and painted for our taste, best (or worst) illustrated by the screen in the Great Hall. But in two major rooms he inserted Italian fireplaces of excellent workmanship, altered the three long galleries to their present glorious, though sombre, appearance, and devised the first staircase in England to mount round a large open well.

The best thing in Knole is left till last – the King's Bedroom. It is not known that any king actually occupied it, but it was furnished with regal splendour in the seventeenth century with silver tables

*The entrance front of Knole – seen here from the park – forms one side of its Green Court; it was built as an extension to the Archbishop's palace by Henry VIII. Thomas Sackville added the gables in about 1605, each surmounted by a Sackville leopard, softening the severity of the front.*

and mirrors, a bed and matching stools. It is the bed that arouses in every visitor a gasp of admiration and surprise. Recently restored, centimetre by centimetre, by a hundred and fifty needlewomen working in teams for thirteen years, its valances, hanging curtains and bedspread, of inter-threaded gold and silver on a coral-coloured satin background, gleam in the low lights. No matter that fear of polluting this precious object has obliged the National Trust to enclose visitors to this room within a transparent box. It is the most splendid piece of furniture in Britain, an awe-striking reminder of the brilliant artistry of an age that we tend to associate with civil war, persecution and debauchery.

Otford Palace is only three miles from Knole, and lies mainly in ruins, but it cannot be disregarded here because it was of prodigious size and outstanding luxury. It was begun in 1514 by another Archbishop of Canterbury, William Warham, who added to the existing great hall and chapel a series of rooms and a vast courtyard of proportions unprecedented in England. Its original extent exceeded that of Hampton Court, its near contemporary. Why the

*Extending for some thousand acres and grazed by a thousand deer, Knole park is the largest private park left in Kent. Its great oaks, beeches and sweet chestnuts suffered severely in the unprecedented hurricane of 16 October 1987.*

Archbishop should need another stupendous mansion when he also owned Knole is unexplained except by his ambition. William Lambarde wrote of him sneeringly, 'He minded to leave to posterity some glorious monument of his worldly wealth and misbegotten treasure.' All that survives is part of the entrance range, now trivialized into cottages, all of brick dressed with stone. Like Knole, it was surrendered by Cranmer to Henry VIII, who astonishingly

*Above: Sarah d'Avigdor Goldsmid of neighbouring Somerhill drowned in a sailing accident; this window to her memory, in All Saints, Tudeley, was designed in 1967 by Marc Chagall.*

*Left: The main border of the rose garden at Sissinghurst.*

abandoned it to four centuries of decay.

If one includes Otford's ruins, Kent's fourth greatest house is undoubtedly Cobham Hall, now a girls' school. It is Elizabethan, begun by William Cobham in 1580, but parts are older, parts later. The south wing, the stateliest, is long and low, its two storeys punctuated at roof level by six great chimneys and terminated at each end by octagonal towers capped by onion domes. The north wing is almost identical, but includes, in contrast to the modest

doorway on the south side, an elaborate porch of 1591, mounting in three stages to the encrusted arms of the Cobham family, all built of the most expensive Caen stone and incorporating classical columns of an accuracy then rare in England. The central block is a mid-seventeenth-century addition, and the service courtyard a century later. In Repton's superb park there is a large mausoleum designed by Wyatt in 1783. Inside the house there is much that was

*Broome Park (c. 1635–8) is the most original seventeenth-century house in Kent. Its dramatic skyline perfectly illustrates the transition from Elizabethan formality to a more experimental English baroque.*

*The garden architecture at Broome Park echoes the main house, its classical features rendered in a homely style: a headless statue stands in a simple brick alcove, and a stone pineapple peeps over the yew hedge.*

remodelled in the early nineteenth century. The architectural centuries are thus all mixed up, unlike Knole, which looks much as it did when Thomas Sackville died in 1608, but Cobham stands as Kent's greatest Elizabethan house, its rich brick absorbing and exuding sunlight. Cobham village is fully worthy of it – a church with the airiest chancel in the county and containing its best brasses and a magnificent Cobham tomb, a fourteenth-century college, and Owletts, a house of cherry-red brick that belonged to Sir Herbert Baker, the architect.

There are many other houses of this early date. One cannot forget the surprise of suddenly passing Hollingbourne Manor on the road to Sittingbourne, with its symmetrical bays and twirly gables, tightly controlled but eternally romantic, nor the two Boughtons, Malherbe and Monchelsea, the first the birthplace of Sir Henry Wotton, the second stone and battlemented, both poised on the greensand ridge overlooking the Weald, exceptions to the rule that the Elizabethans were indifferent to views. The gatehouse of Lullingstone Castle is also sixteenth-century, and so is Chillington Manor in the centre of Maidstone, one of the few large houses of this date to occupy a purely urban site. For its strangeness and beauty one cannot omit the misnamed Sissinghurst Castle – misnamed because it was never a castle; strange for its anachronistic brick tower and disjointed buildings, the survivals of a once double-courtyard house (itself a rarity in the mid-sixteenth century – more like a college); and beautiful for its early brickwork and the

famous garden created there in the 1930s by Vita Sackville-West and her husband Harold Nicolson.

From the seventeenth century the greatest houses are Somerhill, Chevening, Broome Park and Lees Court. The last two are the best. Somerhill is seen standing on its wooded hill as one bypasses Tonbridge, a great Jacobean mansion attributed to John Thorpe. It makes more effort to impress than to charm, formally symmetrical, its gables severely triangular peaking to mean finials, and its side windows pinched, but its mottled sandstone varies the texture agreeably and tiny battlements crown the outside door. Chevening,

*Bourne Park, Bishopsbourne, near Canterbury, is the ideal Queen Anne country house. Its windows, pediment and chimneys are in perfect proportion; stone details are enriched by brick; and the Little Stour has been dammed to form a small lake between the meadows.*

*Although this was originally the entrance to Goodnestone Park, the house is now approached from behind. Other alterations have been made since it was built in 1704: the top storey was added later in the eighteenth century, and the pediment resited above it, to create new but equally satisfying proportions.*

now the Foreign Secretary's equivalent to Chequers, was built about 1625 as Kent's first reaction to Inigo Jones, who may have had a part in designing it. It was a brick house later covered by encaustic tiles, standing below (typically not on) the North Downs, tall for its width, much fenestrated and severely rectilinear. It was twice re-shaped in the eighteenth century, not to its advantage, but it has been excellently restored in recent years and still contains its original saloon, panelled in oak from floor to ceiling.

The exterior of Broome Park, in the hidden country north-west of Folkestone, is unadulterated even by conversion into a residential club and its park into a golf course (after all, Knole and Leeds have one too). Its elaborate brickwork, cut like stone to shape the swirling gables and tall pilasters, express the culmination of the Jacobean style, though it was begun as late as 1635. Inside, there are more changes. Lord Kitchener of Khartoum bought the house in his years of fame, and with the advice of Lady Sackville, herself no mean modernizer of Knole, he replaced the lower flights of the staircase by others brought from Essex and inserted two vast chimneypieces in the hall. But it is the dignity of the great façades

that remains in the mind, the ladderlike ascent of the mullioned windows, the fantastic skyline, the noble chimneys, the rose-pink brick, and the serenity that comes from traditional design adventurously employed. It is undoubtedly Kent's finest seventeenth-century house.

Bolder but not less pleasing is Lees Court (*c*.1650) which makes use of giant Ionic pilasters, standing, fourteen of them, like a silent guard of honour across the long low width of its south front, and although the interior was totally remodelled after a 1912 fire, this marvellous façade by an unknown architect remains, with Mereworth, the great exception to Kent's reputation for architectural conservatism. There is no house in Britain to compare with it for placidity and distinction. In contrast, Groombridge Place (1655), ruled off from Sussex by a stream, is utterly domestic yet by no means simple, for it stands within a moat and has a portico of Ionic columns rising to a pediment. The wonder is that so classical a frontispiece fits in with so very English a composition. Its garden, contained within stone walls contemporary with the earlier fifteenth-century house, mounts in a series of terraces, with yew hedges sheltering little orchards and lawns. Finally, from the seventeenth century, there are the Red House (1686) in Sevenoaks, brick and nobly formal, and Squerries Court, both of which anticipate by their clean symmetry the elegance of the eighteenth.

From that century we have an outburst of new domestic building. First there is Bourne Park (1701), glimpsed suddenly across the valley of the Little Stour as a surprising note of distinction in a district of modest villages. Its near contemporary, Waldershare, a grand Queen Anne house fronted by Corinthian pilasters, was gutted by fire in 1913 and the interior rebuilt by Sir Reginald Blomfield. The best that survive from the early part of the century are Chilston Park, now a luxury hotel, Goodnestone, where Jane Austen began her first version of *Pride and Prejudice*, and especially Bradbourne, near West Malling, the ideal of a Queen Anne house, in texture and proportions so satisfying that one offers silent thanks to the unknown architect for the pleasure he has bequeathed.

Then we come to Finchcocks, which John Newman calls 'the most notable Baroque house in the county', but that, he warns us, is not saying much, for Kent was antipathetic to the Baroque, and the house's chief merit is the view of it from Goudhurst, lying among hop-gardens and woods flung like garlands against the bosomy hills. Godmersham is equally well sited, in a landscaped park ascending the Downs between Ashford and Canterbury, a

*Finchcocks, near Goudhurst, in early September, when half the hop garden has been stripped. The house dates from the 1720s, and rises above its farm buildings in a great cliff of brick.*

113

*Mereworth Castle, Kent's most original house, is a startling but wholly
sympathetic addition to the architecture of the Weald. It was designed in the
1720s by Colen Campbell, under the strong influence of Palladio, and it is closely
modelled on his Villa Rotonda in Vicenza. The pavilions on each side were added
in about 1740, perhaps by 'Athenian' Stuart.*

Built in 1732, with later additions and alterations, Godmersham Park on the
Great Stour is still essentially the house known by Jane Austen when she was
writing the first version of Pride and Prejudice. The house was inherited by her
brother, and her fictional accounts of life in a great country house were much
influenced by her frequent visits here and to Goodnestone.

Brasted Place was built by Robert Adam in swarthy limestone in the late
eighteenth century. Elements of this garden front are exquisite – the proportions,
and the details of the paired Ionic columns and pilasters – but the addition of the
service wing (to the left) in 1871 was a great architectural misfortune.

mansion of great beauty which belonged to Jane Austen's brother, Edward Knight, and where she stayed often. Linton stands overlooking the Weald south of Maidstone, and from the Weald it is one of the few houses on the greensand ridge which catches the eye, for it is stuccoed and painted dead white.

Next comes Mereworth Castle. This is something very special. Anything less like a castle cannot be conceived. It was designed in 1720 by Colen Campbell for John Fane, later seventh Earl of Westmorland, as an adaptation of the Rotonda, or Villa Capra, which Palladio built in the mid-sixteenth century near Vicenza. It was an extraordinarily bold and successful innovation for Kent, a square block of two storeys surmounted by a dome and faced by identical Ionic porticos on each of the four sides. On each flank, framing the frontal view from the road, are exquisite pavilions added in 1740. Though the structure is very solid, Mereworth seems to float. The dome might be gas-filled, tethered to its square base. Inside, it forms a half-egg hall, sumptuously decorated by plaster-work, with a gallery ringing it at the level of the first floor. A house that could seem freakish in this Wealden context is immediately

*Above: Pleached limes standing along the terrace of Brasted Place.*

*Right: Scotney Castle, near Lamberhurst, comprises three parts: Anthony Salvin's house of 1837 stands on a hill above the near perfect fourteenth-century tower and the ruins of the seventeenth-century house attached to it. Looking down from the Salvin house along the shrub- and tree-filled valley, from which its stone was quarried, the eye is drawn to this romantic group of older buildings.*

*Above: The Italian Garden at Hever Castle was created by Lord Astor as a setting for the antique sculpture which he had collected over many years. This Roman statue of Venus and Cupid overlooks the Half-moon Pond.*

*Left: The entrance gateway and outside walls of Hever Castle date from the fourteenth century. Behind them lies a Tudor-style 'village' of interconnecting cottages, which was built by William Waldorf Astor to accommodate his guests, when he bought the castle in 1903.*

recognizable as a great work of art. It is a remarkable incident in the long flirtation between Italy and the Gothic north, as is the nearby church of St Lawrence, built in 1744–6, an astonishing transplantation of a Wren-like city church to a humble village.

Coming to the later eighteenth century, there are two houses assigned to Robert Adam. Mersham-le-Hatch (1762), which was his first completed house, and, more exciting, Brasted Place (1784), built of swarthy sandstone with a noble four-columned porch.

In the nineteenth century, Scotney Castle deserves the palm for its Salvin house built high over a dipping view to an ancient moated castle, now ruinous, and for the shrub and tree garden which has filled the intervening valley, the three in combination forming a landscape which seems drawn from Salvator Rosa. But most large Victorian houses in Kent, as elsewhere, were designed to impress more by size and sumptuousness. As the railways penetrated the county (the first, in 1842, dead straight from Reigate to Ashford), every part of it was accessible in one-and-a-half hours from London, and houses of the newly rich began to proliferate. We had, for instance, Hemsted House, now Benenden School, which in 1859 replaced an Elizabethan house in a bastard Elizabethan style;

Betteshanger, enormous and fake antique, a medley of different materials, styles and date, with connected but unrelated buildings placed at jutting angles, and with frequent changes of level inside; St Alban's Court, also by George Devey, more regularly 'Elizabethan'; Preston Hall, near Aylesford, grimly Jacobean; Bedgebury Park, originally nineteenth-century classical, later transformed into a sort of French Renaissance chateau; and Hall Place, Leigh, another vast and pompous Devey House, built for a hosiery millionaire and now partly demolished.

After all this, it is a relief to come to Lutyens (The Salutation at Sandwich, Great Maytham at Rolvenden, and Wittersham), and finally to Hever Castle and Chartwell.

Where should Hever be placed in this chronology? The oldest part is undoubtedly fourteenth-century, and two centuries later the Boleyns built within the old walls a Tudor mansion where Henry VIII courted his second wife, Anne. It fell into disrepair but never ruin, until in 1903 it was bought by William Waldorf Astor, who restored the fabric, made out of the carcass beautiful modern rooms, and added behind them (all this to justify the nineteenth-century date for the whole) a large 'village' of connected Tudor-style 'cottages' for the accommodation of his guests. Outside the moat he created a garden of amazing luxury and refinement, and a lake of thirty-five acres dug by eight hundred navvies in nineteen months. Hever is not a fake. The stone towers and walls of the main castle are little altered, and the entrance gateway is one of the most romantic sights in England. The interior is a triumph of Edwardian ingenuity and opulent craftsmanship, and the whole complex a tribute to a lonely, elderly American who found solace in saving and embellishing an historic relic of incomparable worth.

Chartwell is of course justly renowned among twentieth-century houses, not for its buildings but for its owner. Winston Churchill chose it for his country house because of its situation at the head of a valley (more like a combe) near Westerham, where his statue sits on the green alongside that of General Wolfe, which stands. Chartwell was rebuilt in 1923 to make the best of the view, and internally owes more to Lady Churchill's taste than to her husband's, for it is bright, chintzy and domesticated, apart from his study and the tiny bedroom off it, which reveal his sturdier, more baronial, personality. The garden too, is Churchillian, with his famous wall, studio, cascade and duck-pond. Future generations will visit this undistinguished house with a curiosity that in time will become faintly numinous.

*Topiary work at Hever Castle.*

# 5

# *Canterbury and the Inland Towns*

THERE ARE MANY towns in Kent, but only two cities, Canterbury and Rochester. The towns spread along the northern coast, tightly packed at the Medway estuary to form a virtual conurbation, prolonged round what one might apologetically call 'holiday corner', and resume at Deal with another intensely built-over coast that extends, with a few gaps, as far as Hythe. Inland, there are five major towns, Maidstone, Ashford, Sevenoaks, Tonbridge and Tunbridge Wells. Of all these towns and cities, there is no doubt which is pre-eminent, Canterbury, for its situation, its historical significance, its cathedral and other medieval buildings, and its contemporary vigour in commerce and the arts.

Let us come to the city, in imagination if not on foot, by its traditional approach, the Pilgrims' Way. It is a trackway beaten out by primitive people and their cattle long before the Roman invasions, and was never developed except here and there into a metalled road. It runs from Winchester to Canterbury just below the North Downs, intermediate between the wooded crest and the valley, and through Surrey and Kent it can still be defined, rising, falling, clinging. It was not the route which Chaucer's pilgrims took, since they rode from Southwark along Watling Street, but for millennia it was the principal thoroughfare east from Salisbury Plain, joined at Canterbury by the short spurs that led from the Channel ports. After Becket's murder and canonization it acquired its present name.

It is a beautiful path, sometimes a lane, rarely diverted by later buildings or parks (one exception is Chevening's), taking the rivers in its stride – the Darent at Otford, the Medway at Snodland – and it comes to Canterbury, above Charing and Godmersham and through pretty Chilham, between orchards and hop gardens and along the edges of hanging woods, till at Harbledown the pilgrims (among them Erasmus) obtained their first view, now unhappily

*Previous page: Canterbury from the north. The view is dominated by the cathedral and the roofs of King's School, on the nearer side of the cathedral walls.*

*Right: Beeches in springtime along the Pilgrims' Way, north of Charing.*

obscured, of Canterbury Cathedral. The sound of the bells saluted them. It is said that they fell to their knees in ecstasy.

You have just passed through Bigbury Camp which Caesar captured in 54 BC. It is now conjectured that Bigbury was the main settlement of the Belgic people hereabouts, but that Canterbury already existed as an Iron Age village beside the Stour. The Romans abandoned Bigbury, like many other places – the best-known example is their switch from Maiden Castle to Dorchester – for the

*Much of St Martin's church, Canterbury, is constructed of Roman brick, and it almost certainly already existed as a Christian chapel when St Augustine first preached here in 597. It can legitimately claim to be the cradle of English Christianity.*

swampy ground beside the river, where it could be forded and ships could approach from Richborough at least as far as neighbouring Fordwich. They built at Canterbury Kent's major town, and called it *Durovernum Cantiacorum*, derived from the British words *duro* (fort) and *verno* (swamp). It was in fact unfortified till the late third century AD, when the walls were built. The many traces of Roman Canterbury – a mosaic pavement here, a chunk of masonry there, some materials re-used in later churches like St Martin's and St Mildred's, the grassy burial mound in Dane John Gardens – were either re-buried after excavation, or are so scattered that it is impossible to gain an impression of Roman Canterbury without a chart or guide. Some stones on the south side of the castle wall are Roman, and in 1986 archaeologists uncovered the Ridingate where Watling Street entered, an impressive double gateway flanked by guard chambers. Within the city many of the Roman remains were disinterred when rebuilding began after the severe destruction of the Second World War, and excavation has continued ever since as different parts are laid open for the construction of new commercial buildings and car parks. Like an underlying ghost town, the plan of Roman Canterbury has slowly been revealed. The evidence suggests that it was a wealthy town of about a hundred and twenty acres, extending to a suburb beyond its walls. It was a commercial and administrative centre, but not until the last phase a garrison town. It was probably laid out in a grid pattern of streets, of which one was Burgate, a little south of the cathedral, with another at right angles to it, lined by well-built houses of stone and timber. Near the town centre was an open-air theatre, larger than the only other British example at St Albans, and a forum surrounded by basilicas, and there were two bath buildings.

Canterbury enjoyed a long period of peace under Roman rule, and became the capital of Kent's pagan, later Christian, kings. Of St Augustine's great Benedictine Abbey, built outside the city walls, only some foundations remain exposed, unappealing and almost inexplicable except by experts, but the blitzed site of it is of intense historical interest as a relic of the very beginning of Anglo-Saxon Christianity. Bede records its building in 598 as a monastery 'of becoming splendour . . . in which church the body of Augustine and also those of all bishops and kings of Canterbury might be laid'. There was not one Saxon church within the precinct but four, three of which were pulled down just after the Norman Conquest to make room for a fifth on an even larger scale. This survived until the Reformation, when it was obliterated by a palace built for Henry VIII. The earliest of the Saxon churches, dedicated to St Peter and St Paul in 613, was built partly of Roman bricks, and the site of Augustine's tomb is known, west of the altar against the north wall,

but his shrine was moved to the Norman church, and at the Dissolution to Chilham. In the precincts a gateway, called Fyndon Gate, was raised early in the fourteenth century, a heavily enriched two-turreted gatehouse with a wide archway, much damaged by bombing in 1942 but carefully restored.

Canterbury Cathedral was founded by St Augustine as a small church dedicated to Christ himself. Nothing of it survives, nor of a second church built by Cuthbert in the mid-eighth century. Larger and larger churches were erected on the site as need arose, or tragedy struck in the form of fires or Danish raids. Again in 1067 the cathedral was burnt to the ground, and when Lanfranc came to Canterbury as Archbishop in 1070, all he found was a heap of ruins. Within seven years he built an enormous Benedictine church and conventual precincts for a hundred and fifty monks. These too have disappeared, and the earliest surviving work is the shell of the choir and east transept, built on a vast scale over a spacious crypt by Lanfranc's successor, Anselm, and rebuilt after another fire in 1174, only four years after the murder of Thomas Becket.

Some account must be given of this extraordinary man, for it is to him that we owe not the cathedral itself but its sudden resurgence.

*The gateway known as Fyndon Gate forms the entrance to St Augustine's College in Canterbury. It was built originally in 1300 but has been much restored since 1942, when it suffered heavy war damage.*

*The ambulatory of the Norman crypt in Canterbury Cathedral is the largest and best-lit crypt in England. Having survived the fire of 1174, it is still remarkably well-preserved.*

His martyrdom was the most important single event in Kent's history.

He was described by a contemporary as 'blithe of countenance, winning and loveable in all conversation but slightly stuttering in his talk, keen in discernment and of a wondrously strong memory'. Such a paragon was soon elevated by Henry II to high rank in Church and State, and Becket even led in battle seven hundred knights to capture Toulouse. The king's close reliance on him, and their friendship, began to falter when Becket, now raised to archbishop, displayed increasing arrogance and defiance of the Crown, using his powers to deprive half the bishops of their offices and threatening to excommunicate the king himself. Henry responded by exiling Becket, who returned to Canterbury six years later, angered to the point of hysteria and determined to prove by his own martyrdom the independence of the Church from royal authority. 'I go to England,' he said, 'to die.' He had antagonized almost all the clerics, but the people stood behind him. When he landed from France at Sandwich, many ran into the sea and knelt in the shallow water, crying, 'Blessed is he who cometh in the name of the Lord!'

Becket, fortified by this support, and as truculent as ever,

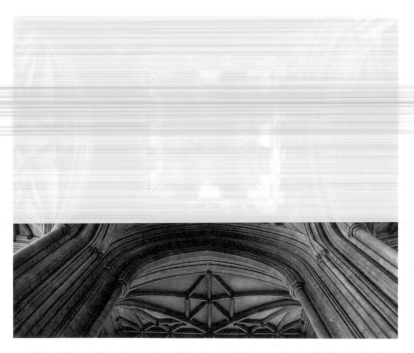

*Above: The crossing of the nave and transepts under Canterbury Cathedral's central tower combines the styles of two periods – early Perpendicular and the more florid fan-vaulting of a century later.*

*Right: Canterbury Cathedral from the south-east. The central tower – 'Bell Harry' – was completed c.1498 and has been called the noblest Gothic tower in existence; to the left lies the great length of the nave (1410); the south-east transept, with its rose window, dates from nearly two centuries earlier.*

denounced the king from the pulpit, excommunicated the bishops of London and Salisbury, and suspended the Archbishop of York. When news of this reached Henry, he exploded with words that have become immortal, 'Of the caitiffs who eat my bread, are there none to free me of this turbulent priest?' The response was immediate. Four knights met at Saltwood Castle to plot Becket's murder. The scene is well recorded. On 29 December 1170 Becket entered the cathedral from the cloisters by a door into the north transept, pursued by the knights. When the monks attempted to close the door, he re-opened it with his own hands, crying, 'I am here, no traitor to the king, but a priest. Why do ye seek me?' As one of the knights lifted his sword, Becket bowed his head to receive the blow. Another scattered his brains over the pavement. At the very site of this appalling crime, Archbishop Runcie and Pope John Paul II knelt side by side on 29 May 1982. He was the first Pope ever to visit Great Britain.

After the fire of 1174, only the crypt, the nave and the eastern towers were left intact. The choir was rebuilt by the master mason William of Sens. It was later extended by the Trinity Chapel to contain Becket's tomb, which for the next three centuries became an object of veneration by pilgrims from all over the known world. In the late fourteenth century the nave was rebuilt from the profits of the pilgrimages in the new Perpendicular style, and the chapter house and the cloisters remodelled. The two west transepts are fifteenth century, as is the great central Bell Harry Tower which dominates not just the cathedral but the city. Thus was formed in essentials the great church we see today.

Its different building styles in no way jar upon today's visitors,
for our eyes have become so accustomed to the general thrust of Gothic architecture that its periods, which must have seemed revolutionary when one succeeded another, now appear as the achievement of a single intention. The change of mood from nave to choir is simply what one expects with the change of function, and the transition is emphasized by the difference of levels, steps leading upwards between them, and up again to the Trinity Chapel. The eye constantly follows the shafts of piers and columns to their graceful webbing on the ceilings, especially in the nave, the chapter house (where T.S.Eliot's *Murder in the Cathedral* was first performed), and the Trinity Chapel, then descends to the window glass, the tombs (the Black Prince recumbent in full armour) and St Augustine's chair, thirteenth-century, still used for the enthronement of archbishops. From outside, and especially from the high ground where Kent University has sited its campus, the cathedral is a wonderfully light building for all its immensity, its great length suspended from three pale towers. Any risk of monotony is avoided by the buttresses, finials and ornamental windows, piece added unfalteringly to piece until the east end terminates in a graceful semi-circular chapel known appropriately as the Corona or Becket's Crown.

The cathedral is of course Canterbury's main attraction. It is the only place in Kent to draw more than a million visitors a year, apart from Margate's amusement park. In the rest of the city there are medieval and Tudor buildings in profusion – like the King's School under the cathedral walls, built around its own green, the Westgate's drum towers which still flank one of the main entrances to the city, small chapels, large churches, inns, monumental gateways like that which admits you to the cathedral close, the ruins of the castle and the fine circumvallation of the city walls. Post-medieval centuries added little except timbered houses, and most survived until German raids destroyed much of the town, without touching the cathedral. The shattered parts were rebuilt in modern

*Wingham and Ickham are two satellite villages near Canterbury. Wingham, above, lies on the Roman road from Richborough and is marked by the distinctive green spire of St Mary's church. Ickham, a lovely church to be married in, is plain, but finely proportioned, with a tapering, shingled broach spire.*

dress to suit modern needs, one traffic-free street lined by supermarkets, other areas surrendered to parked cars, nothing remarkable, little offensive, and none on a scale to dispute the cathedral's supremacy. It is a place vibrant with tourists and shoppers, which manages to absorb them all without surprise and exude them without fuss. The transient traffic is diverted by outer roads. The one failing is that Canterbury ignores its river, the reason why the city was sited here in the first place. Apart from one pretty riverside garden, the Stour is allowed to bifurcate into hidden channels and creep away unloved.

Rochester I will leave till the last chapter, as it forms the keystone of the north Kent arch of towns, and come directly to Maidstone, the county's capital. Canterbury would have made a more historic capital, but it is too devotional and too cramped for space, while Maidstone has such ample space that it is spreading in great whorls into the surrounding country, threatening to collar villages like East Barming, Loose, Sandling and Bearsted in its grasp, and throwing out new estates with such rapidity that the Ordnance Survey is hard pressed to keep pace.

Maidstone is not an attractive town. It has a middle but no centre. The wide main street descends a gentle hill to the Medway, but it has been spoiled by bad building in the last hundred and fifty years, and the bridge, instead of being a feature, is a flat extension of the road, doubled in recent years to ease the traffic and pilot it round a complicated series of roundabouts. Once the motorist has been ejected from this vortex into the town, he finds himself twisted this way and that by the most awkward one-way street system in England except Oxford's.

However, if you take to your feet, you will find pleasant surprises. One is Mote Park, a large eighteenth-century house, now a Cheshire Home, and the park itself, with a great lake formed by the damming of the River Len, has been thrown open for public recreation. It approaches quite closely the centre of Maidstone, and most of it is left in its original condition. Apart from litter, benches and notices like 'No night fishing', it is a brave attempt to adapt a patrician estate to communal enjoyment. The other surprise is a group of medieval buildings beside the Medway. Here Maidstone proclaims its ancestry. There is first the parish church of All Saints, the grandest Perpendicular church in Kent, and nearby the old Palace of the Archbishops. Beyond the church lies Archbishop Courtenay's College, with a fine gate tower, and opposite the Palace, the old episcopal stables, now housing an exhibition of coaches.

These grey buildings, especially when viewed from across the

*All Saints, Maidstone, is the grandest fourteenth-century church in Kent. In the foreground are the medieval choir stalls, and beyond, looking towards the west end, lies the twelve-arched nave.*

Medway, form a group which shames the rest of central Maidstone. Here and there you will find a few other relics of the past, like St Peter's, a thirteenth-century chapel, a couple of pargetted houses, and Chillington Manor, the borough's unworthy museum (what Kent deserves is a county museum of top quality), but it takes much imagination to recreate Maidstone's appearance when Celia Fiennes visited it in 1697, and found 'several pretty streets'. No street is any longer pretty. When one compares a beautiful eighteenth-century house like Romney House to its modern neighbour, one despairs that there is nothing here that visitors two centuries hence will come to look at with pleasure. Except, perhaps, one building, the new Crown Court, which stands boldly on the river bank beside the bridge, taking pride in its situation, materials and design. And one must admit that for all the insensitive rebuilding, this is still what Defoe found, 'a town of very great business and trade, and yet full of gentry, of mirth and good company'. Maidstone is by no means impoverished or glum.

Nor is Ashford. This is the one town in Kent which is bound to benefit from the Channel Tunnel. It will have an international

*Above: One of Maidstone's Methodist chapels is a distinguished early nineteenth-century building in a town largely ruined by later Victorian additions.*

*Left: The Archbishops' Palace, seen from across the Medway. It was built of locally quarried Kentish ragstone at the end of the fourteenth century and now stands – solid and serene – in the middle of busy and ever-growing Maidstone, Kent's capital town.*

railway station with trains running direct to European cities and an Inland Clearance Depot for customs checks. It is so well linked by road and rail to the rest of England that it has the potential to become the manufacturing and commercial hub of the region, 'radiating confidence and opportunity to less resilient areas', as an official study puts it, thinking perhaps of Dover, Folkestone and the Medway towns. In case this prospect alarms Ashford's less resilient inhabitants, they are assured that it will not become a monster growth. The surrounding country will be slightly encroached upon and there will be a rise in property values, but the new housing estates, factories and warehousing will have a 'campus-like' decorum, the study euphemistically predicts, giving architects and town planners opportunities that have been badly neglected in Kent since the war. 'Means should be found,' it says, 'to give the borough a higher profile and a clear identity.'

Most strangers bypass Ashford to join the M20, and find in its

rambling industrial outskirts little to attract them inside. They are missing a lot. It has several medieval and eighteenth-century houses and a handsome church, St Mary's, and Ashford is not without its famous sons. Jack Cade, the rebel, came from here, and so did John Wallis, the great mathematician, born in the year that Shakespeare died. At the heart of the town there are reminders of the Ashford they knew, a nest of short streets, with jettied houses almost touching across narrow alleys. It is a busy sort of place, an updated market town, but it suffered in the mid-nineteenth century when it became an important railway junction, and an ugly new district was built to house the employees of the engine works. The River Stour, as in Canterbury, is denied its deserts as a much needed amenity. To canoe its dirty waters through the town, as I have done, is a penance to be endured before reaching the beautifully cut valleys to the north, floating past lovely Wye, and at the foot of three great houses, Olantigh, Godmersham and Chilham.

Sevenoaks is sweeter and smarter than Ashford. First, on its immediate outskirts it has Knole and its park, the largest in Kent,

*Hinxhill church, near Ashford, is basically thirteenth century, but the north aisle, seen here, was added a century later.*

*The sheep market at Ashford specialises in the sale of Romney Marsh sheep. The town has retained the air of an agricultural market town, although it is mainly a shopping and industrial centre, with a railway station soon to be enlarged as a base for Channel Tunnel traffic.*

and just off the centre of the town, the Vine, a cricket ground of beauty and surprising antiquity: it was here that the Duke of Dorset led his estate workers to defeat an All England team in 1782 for the astonishingly high stake of a thousand guineas. The old road from Tonbridge, now happily bypassed by the A21, S-bends at the entrance to the town to reveal suddenly an exceptionally broad street with, on one side, the school designed by Lord Burlington and on the other St Nicholas, opposite the unassuming entrance to Knole, where John Donne was rector and William Lambarde is buried. Next, the High Street gives another wiggle and opens up to the town's centre where the road bifurcates, to the right the main shops and beyond them the Vine, to the left a less animated thoroughfare that leads downhill to the swimming baths and the station. Nearly all the streets have an assortment of old houses like the Chantry, Vine House, the Red House and the Old Vicarage, that give them much grace, and the slow fall of the roads, the leafy, winding suburbs, moderate the inevitable congestion of commercial activity in the middle. Sevenoaks is a commuters' town. A third of its working population travel daily to London. Green Belt

*Above: The castle at Tonbridge, which guards the ford over the Medway, was one of the first castles to be built after the Norman Conquest. There was originally a motte, and the massive stone gatehouse was built about 1300, with a great hall on its upper floor. The motte survives bereft of its buildings, and beside the castle is a Georgian house.*

*Left: Pollarded willow trees near Wye.*

restrictions have kept it confined, and property values have soared. In its surroundings are great houses and gardens like Riverhill and Emmetts and, on the slopes of the Downs, St Clere and Chevening. Between them we find smaller and more recent houses hidden between the hills and woods and up the Darent valley, which has been revealed, not ruined, by the M25.

Tonbridge Castle has been described in previous pages. It is much the most interesting building in the town, and its motte a phenomenal survival. The Medway flows cleanly beneath the High Street, which opens up beyond the bridge to give breathing space to Tonbridge School, mostly Victorian Gothic. The best of the houses is Ferox Hall, 1740, on the other side of the High Street, facing the school. Tonbridge is unusual for being, in essence, just this one street, and its extensions along the railway to one side, and to a complex of supermarkets on the other, do little to make this

but long since abandoned to the railway. The middle of the town again suffers from having been designated a main traffic route since the Romans. Across a mercifully empty stretch of countryside between all this urbanization, we come to Gravesend. It has grown enormously in size, but has lost most of the river traffic which gave it fame when passengers disembarked here to continue their journey by road to east Kent and the Channel ports, and incoming vessels first touched land. Today only lighters moor against the town quay, but there is a patient ferry which crosses to Tilbury, and long slim ships slide occasionally down the tideway.

If you take the ferry and look back at the Gravesend shore, you see an unbroken line of wharfs, a few of them derelict, most still active, great chimneys belching smoke, and, pricking the skyline, the spire of an unexpected eighteenth-century church. This is St George's, which was rebuilt in 1727 by a local carpenter after a fire, and reveals by its clumsiness his ignorance of the Wren tradition. It is worth visiting for one reason, Pocahontas. She was the Indian princess, the daughter of Powhatan who ruled over the part of Virginia which English settlers colonized in 1607, and married one of them, John Rolfe. He brought her back to England from Jamestown, and she enjoyed at Court considerable notoriety for her exotic beauty, but falling sick and longing for her own country, in 1617 she persuaded her husband to return with her to Virginia. They got no further than Gravesend. There she landed, died aged only 23, and was buried in the chancel of old St George's. Her grave was destroyed by the fire, but her bronze statue, a replica of that at Jamestown, was placed in the churchyard in 1957, the 350th anniversary of the founding of the colony. She looks towards the river, sprightly, slim, perhaps idealized, the most sentimental token in this very unsentimental place.

Northfleet comes next, at the point where the Thames ceases to be an estuary and becomes a river. There is an ancient lane that leads down to a wharf with pub and cottages, a surprisingly rural nook of this industrial shore. Nearby, at Greenhythe, the Empire Mills delight by their modern design, and there is one old church, at Stone, which has been recognized as one of the most beautiful in Kent. John Newman, who is not given to hyperbole, calls it 'unforgettable'. He dates it from 1260 on the evidence of panels identical in character to some in Westminster Abbey of the same date. The rather dull exterior does not prepare the visitor for the springing arcades of the nave and the refinement of the carving. It is a remarkably elaborate building to find in what was then a tiny village, and the suspicion grows that it was built by Lawrence de St Martin, Bishop of Rochester, who was chaplain to Henry III and shared his artistic taste.

*Stone, near Dartford, on Kent's north-west boundary, has a thirteenth-century church, built by masons who had worked on Westminster Abbey. The modest exterior of the church does not lead the visitor to expect the abundance of high-quality sculpture and fittings to be found inside.*

Finally we come to Dartford. Since 1965 the county boundary separates it from Erith, Crayford and Bexley, which with Bromley are now part of Greater London, and meets the Thames just north of the town, where the Darent enters the main stream. Dartford has a few old houses of which it has made a good display, but it is in the main industrial, and is striving energetically to revive its prosperity after an interval of slump. For this it has great advantages, its access to the Thames and a key situation alongside the M25, which at this point plunges under the river through road-tunnels, soon to be supplemented by a vast road bridge. There are proposals to develop the worked-out chalk quarries, to turn the low land into factory sites and marinas, and to build new housing estates on derelict land. Evidence of this major re-thinking is already apparent on the ground, and although Dartford cannot be said to be typical of Kent, it plays an important part in the county's resurgence and is a facet of its history no less significant than the prettier small towns and villages of the Weald.

# Index